TABLE OF CONTENTS

A Note to Students

Thomas Edison once said that genius is "one percent inspiration and ninety-nine percent perspiration." By that he meant that success is due more often to hard work and effort than to natural or innate abilities. Nearly all students can be academically successful if they study and, more importantly, know how to study.

The purpose of this study guide is to help you better understand the material presented in your textbook, *Child Development: Change Over Time,* and to help you prepare for exams. Various exercises have been prepared for each chapter that are intended to reinforce important points and to test you knowledge and understanding of the material. First, an overview of each chapter has been provided to emphasize key points and concepts. Second, a brief chapter outline has been provided for you to use as a study tool. You may find it useful to write notes that include important facts or concepts in the margins of the outline. Third, a list of terms, concepts and vocabulary words for you to define and memorize has been included for each chapter. Fourth, review questions have been provided that cover important points from each chapter. Answering the review questions as thoroughly and completely as possible is an excellent way to prepare for exams and is strongly recommended. Finally, practice exercises have been included to help you test your knowledge of the material that you have read in each chapter. The mix-and-match items are intended to test your knowledge of the key definitions and terms that you have learned. The practice tests include a sample of multiple choice, true and false and fill-in-the-blank items similar to what you may have on an exam.

By using this study guide, you have taken an important step toward academic success. But in addition to completing the exercises in this study guide, the development of good study skills is equally important to your success in college. Listed below are some recommended guidelines for developing study habits that can facilitate your academic success.

Find a quiet place where you can study uninterrupted. Have your ever read a chapter from a textbook only to realize that you couldn't remember anything you had read? Perhaps it's because your environment interfered with you ability to study. Settings that are noisy and disruptive can interfere with a student's concentration and ability to understand material. If your family or roommates are distracting you from your studies, try to find a quiet place, such as the school library, where you won't be disturbed.

Include regular study periods in your weekly schedule. Planning and adhering to regular study periods is vital to student success. If you work full or part time, try to establish a school schedule that is realistic and compatible with your work schedule. Students sometimes fail to realize that to be successful, school should be considered a full time job. It is recommended that students set aside approximately three hours of study time for every hour spent inside of the classroom. Therefore, you should prepare a work and study schedule at the beginning of the semester and try to follow the schedule as closely as possible.

Alternate the topics during your study period. Some students find that studying for two highly similar topics back-to-back, such as biology and the biological aspects of human sexuality, interferes with their ability to remember the source from which the information came. To avoid any such confusion, try to alternate the topics that you study

Study Guide

CH[...]GE

HarperCollins *CollegePublishers*

Study Guide to accompany Newcombe, CHILD DEVELOPMENT: CHANGE OVER TIME 8E

ISBN: 0-673-99332-9

96 97 98 99 00 9 8 7 6 5 4 3 2 1

so that you do not study two similar topics in a row. For example, you could study American history in between biology and human sexuality. By doing so, you can separate the material that you have learned and reduce the likelihood that you will confuse the material later.

Read and highlight important information in the textbook. You may find it useful to underline or highlight information as you read a chapter. Highlighting key concepts or writing notes to yourself in the margins of the textbook may help you retain some of the more important material covered in the chapter.

Practice writing essays in advance. There is an unfortunate tendency for students to believe that writing is a natural talent with which an individual is born. The fact is that writing well is due more to practice and hard work than to innate ability. When preparing an essay, try to organize it in a logical and meaningful order so that your response can be easily understood by the reader. In addition, providing examples or citing relevant studies from the textbook is a good way to emphasize important points you want to make in your essay. You may also find it useful to outline and memorize your final essay answer so that you won't forget to include any important information on the day of the exam. As painful as it may be, writing an essay is an excellent way for you to understand the material you have studied. If you can't explain the material, you may not understand it as well as you thought you did. If you can it clearly and concisely, you probably understand it!

Find a study partner. Some students find that it helps to study with one or two other students from their class. Study groups provide students with the opportunity to share class notes, quiz each other on course material, and clarify material that one or more students may not understand. Although I highly recommend study groups, I suggest that you limit a study group to no more than two or three students. Large study groups tend to be less organized and may turn into more of a social hour than a study session.

I hope that this study guide and the study tips offered above will help you to gain the most out of this course. I can think of no endeavor that is more important than the pursuit of an education nor any topic more important than child development. I encourage you to do your best to succeed and wish you the best of luck in this and all courses you take during your college years.

CHAPTER 1:
THEORY AND METHOD IN THE STUDY OF CHILD DEVELOPMENT

CHAPTER OVERVIEW

The study of child development focuses on the physical, psychological, emotional, and social changes that occur as children grow and mature. One important goal of developmental research is to identify universal changes that occur in children regardless of culture. Another important goal is to better understand individual differences to improve parenting and discipline strategies. A third goal is to understand the way in which environmental context affects a child's behavior. Identifying universal changes, as well as the way in which individual and environmental influences affect behavior, allows researchers to have a more comprehensive understanding of human development.

One important theoretical issue related to child development concerns the relative importance of environmental vs. biological influences on behavior. Environmental determinists argue that a child's environment is the most critical determinant of behavior, whereas biological determinists argue that factors such as genetics and physiological maturation exert a more powerful influence. Another theoretic issue surrounds the role that the children play in their intellectual and social development. Learning theorists argue that children are passive recipients of information, and cognitive theorists argue that children play an active role in their development and have innate tendencies to explore, create and organize their experiences within a mental framework. A third theoretical issue concerns continuity vs. discontinuity in development. Some theorists argue that change is gradual and continuous, whereas other theorists argue that some development is discontinuous and occurs in stages. Finally, research on the stability of behavior and traits over time and across situations has revealed that although children's behavior tends to become more stable and predictable over time, there is considerable variation of behavior across situations.

There are several research methods that are used in the study of development. Cross-sectional research examines developmental changes over time by comparing the abilities of children in various ages groups, but it does not allow the researcher to study transitional changes of individual children, e.g., from physical to verbal aggression. Differences in past experience associated with various age groups also may limit the researcher's overall interpretation of the data. Researchers who use the longitudinal method avoid some of these problems by collecting data from one group of children at regular intervals, allowing them to examine developmental changes that occur over time. However, this method is time-consuming and expensive. Moreover, subjects who move or who drop out of a study may differ significantly from those who do not, which may affect a researcher's interpretation of the data. Finally, there is some concern that repeated testing and "practice" may affect the overall validity of a study's findings.

Whereas cross-sectional and longitudinal research provide information about developmental changes over time, other methods explore questions about cause and effect. Correlations allow researchers to determine whether two variables, e.g., age and cognitive ability, are significantly related to each other but do not provide information about causality. The experimental method is used to establish cause-effect relationships by way of random assignment, systematic manipulation of variables and careful observation of their effects on behavior. However, the artificial environment of the laboratory may limit the extent to which researchers can generalize their findings. Field experiments have the advantage of allowing researchers to manipulate variables and collect data in a more natural environment. Cross-cultural research provides useful information about important differences in development in other countries. Finally, the cross-species method allows researchers to conduct research that would be either difficult or unethical to conduct with humans. Regardless of the method used, developmental researchers adhere to strict ethical guidelines and strive to respect the dignity and privacy of their subjects.

1

CHAPTER OUTLINE: Use the outline provided below by writing information related to each topic in the margins of the outline, e.g., definitions of terms and elaboration of concepts.

I. **What is Development?**

    A.. *Development defined*

    B. *Goals in the study of child development*

II. **Theoretical Issues in Child Development**

    A. *Environmental versus biological determinants of behavior*

    B. *Active versus passive nature of the child*

    C. *Continuity versus discontinuity in development*

    D. *Stability of development over time*

    E. *Consistency of behavior across situations*

III. **Methods of Research on Child Development**

    A. *Cross-sectional investigations*

    B. *Longitudinal investigations*

    C. *Correlational research*

    D. *Experimental research*

    E. *Cross-Cultural and multiethnic studies*

    F. *Cross-species studies*

IV. **Ethical Issues in Research**

    A. *Ethical Problems and concerns*

    B. *Ethical guidelines and principles*

KEY DEFINITIONS AND TERMS: Identify the following terms, concepts and names. Try to provide an example for each word or term you have defined to help clarify its meaning.

Development:

Universal changes:

Individual differences:

Environmental context:

Ecology:

Biological determinants of behavior:

Environmental determinants of behavior:

Transactions:

Stimulus-response learning:

Observational learning:

Active vs. passive learning:

Continuity in development:

Discontinuity in development:

Applied research:

Basic research:

Cross-sectional investigations:

Longitudinal investigation:

Correlational research:

Positive correlation:

Negative correlation:

Experiment:

Independent variable:

Dependent variable:

Random assignment:

Field experiment:

Cross-cultural and multiethnic research:

Cross-species research:

REVIEW QUESTIONS: Below are questions that relate to key concepts and information covered in your textbook. Answer the questions as thoroughly and completely as possible. Try to provide examples to support your answer and to clarify meaning.

1. Describe the three primary goals in the study of development. How can greater knowledge about universal changes, individual differences and contextual and situational influences improve our understanding of child development and behavior?

2. Discuss the "nature versus nurture" controversy and some of the ways in which biological and environmental determinists differ in their explanations of human behavior. What are the major tenets and beliefs of each position?

3. How does learning theory analyze and explain children's development? According to this view, are children active or passive participants in the learning process? What new dimension did social learning theory add to learning theory?

4. Discuss the view taken by cognitive theorists, such as Piaget, that children actively interpret their environment. What assumptions do these theorists have about the child's role in the learning process? What position do learning theorists take?

5. Provide some examples of what developmental psychologists mean when they refer to continuous vs. discontinuous development. What two criterion must be met for a developmental period to be considered a stage? Are "stages" an example of continuous or discontinuous development?

6. Discuss the research that has studied the stability of children's behavior over time. In general, does behavior become more stable or less stable as children grow older? What is meant by the term "functionally equivalent"? Provide an example to support your answer.

7. Describe the cross-sectional and the longitudinal method of research used by developmental psychologists to study changes over time. What are the advantages and disadvantages of each of these research methods?

8. Describe the correlational method of research and the way in which it can be used to study developmental issues. How is correlational research limited in its ability to infer cause and effect relationships between variables?

9. Describe the experimental method of research. How does this method allow researchers to establish causal relationships among variables? Discuss the importance of random assignment and manipulation and control of relevant variables in the experimental method. What are the major advantages and disadvantages of this method?

10. Describe the following methods of research and provide an example of each method: the field experiment, cross-cultural and multiethnic research, and cross-species research. What are the advantages and disadvantages of each of these methods?

MIX-AND-MATCH: In the left-hand column below are some key concepts or definitions. Choose the term from the column on the right that best matches each definition provided in the column on the left.

1. Orderly and relatively enduring changes over time in physical and neurological structures, in thought processes, in emotions, in social interactions and in many other behaviors

2. Theorists who believe human behavior is caused by genetic makeup, physiological maturation, and neurological functioning

3. Theorists who believe that physical and social surroundings are the key determinants shaping behavior

4. Type of development in which rapid and noticeable changes occur

5. Development that is believed to occur in small, gradual, cumulative steps

6. Method of research that investigates relationships between variables but cannot determine a causal relationship

7. Method of research in which children of different ages are compared at one point in time

8. Method of research in which the same children are observed or tested at regular intervals over an extended period of time

9. Method of research in which the investigator systematically changes one or more variables and collects and analyzes changes in another variable

10. Method of research in which subjects are randomly assigned to groups that undergo different experiences but are observed in naturally occurring situations

11. Research that involves comparative studies in other cultures or other ethnic or social class groups

12. Research that employs the use of animals to study developmental processes that are comparable to processes that occur in humans

13. Term used to describe developmental periods that are qualitatively different from each other and occur in a fixed order

a. Experimental method

b. Continuous development

c. Cross-species research

d. Development

e. Field experiment

f. Longitudinal research

g. Cross-cultural research

h. Stages of development

i. Cross-sectional research

j. Biological determinists

k. Discontinuous development

l. Correlational research

m. Environmental determinists

1. Developmental changes that occur in all children regardless of culture are referred to as
   a. fixed.
   b. random.
   c. universal.
   d. ethnocentric.

2. Which of the following statements about child development best resolves the "nature versus nurture" debate?
   a. Biological influences play a far more important role than environmental influences.
   b. Environmental influences play a far more important role than biological influences.
   c. Neither biological nor environmental influences are important in development.
   d. Both biological and environmental influences work together to produce outcomes.

3. Which of the following statements regarding stages of development is false?
   a. Stages involve sudden and discontinuous jumps that produce new patterns of behavior.
   b. Stages occur in a fixed order.
   c. Stages involve small, cumulative, gradual changes in development.
   d. Stages are qualitatively different from each other.

4. Research investigating the stability of children's behavior has revealed that
   a. children's behavior becomes more stable as they grow older.
   b. children's behavior becomes less stable as they grow older.
   c. children's behavior remains stable regardless of the situation.
   d. children's behavior is random and unpredictable regardless of their age.

5. Research intended to generate knowledge about the processes and sequences of development is called
   a. applied research.
   b. basic research.
   c. field research.
   d. general research.

6. Research in which children of different ages are compared at one point in time is called
   a. cross-sectional research.
   b. longitudinal research.
   c. experimental research.
   d. correlational research.

7. The method of research in which children are observed or tested at regular intervals over an extended period is called
   a. cross-sectional research.
   b. longitudinal research.
   c. experimental research.
   d. correlational research.

8. A disadvantage of correlational research is that
   a. it is unable to answer important research questions.
   b. it is too time consuming and costly to conduct.
   c. most researchers consider it to be an "unscientific" method of research.
   d. it does not permit researchers to draw conclusions about cause and effect.

9. The most rigorous way to establish a cause and effect relationship between variables is through the use of
   a. correlational research.
   b. experimental research.
   c. longitudinal research.
   d. cross-sectional research.

10. In an experiment, the variable that the investigator systematically changes is called the
    a. independent variable.
    b. dependent variable.
    c. fixed variable.
    d. random variable.

TRUE AND FALSE QUESTIONS: Read the following statements and indicate whether you think each statement is true or false.

1. Researchers in child development agree that behavior and development are primarily the result of biological influences.

2. Continuous development is sometimes referred to as "stages of development."

3. In general, children's behavior becomes more stable as they grow older.

4. The purpose of applied research is to enable parents, schools and others to deal more effectively with children.

5. Correlational research is an excellent method to use if a researcher is interested in determining a cause and effect relationship between variables.

6. A disadvantage of longitudinal research is that it does not allow the researcher to identify the extent to which individual children undergo transitions from physical to verbal aggression.

7. Cognitive theorists believe that children have an inborn tendency to be curious, to explore their environment, and to organize their experience in their own mental frameworks.

8. Cross-sectional research is an excellent way of determining transitional changes that individual children may undergo.

9. A negative correlation means that two variables are not significantly or statistically related.

10. An advantage of cross-species research is that it can provide useful and valuable information about developmental processes that are comparable to those that occur in humans.

FILL-IN-THE-BLANKS: Read the following sentences and write the missing word or words in the space provided.

1. Three primary goals of development research are to study _____, _____ and _____.

2. Cognitive theorists, such as Piaget, believe that children take an _____ role in their development whereas learning theorists believe that children take a _____ role.

3. The view that a child's physical and social surroundings are the critical determinants of behavior is shared by _____ whereas _____ believe that factors such as genetics and maturation play a more important role.

4. Discontinuous periods of development in which rapid developmental changes occur and which follow a specific order are called _____.

5. Research designed to help parents, schools and others deal with children is called _____ research and research that is intended to generate knowledge about the processes and sequences of development is called _____ research.

6. In an experiment, the variable that is systematically changed by the experimenter is called the _____ and the variable in which objective measurements are taken by the researcher is called the _____ .

7. Research that uses animals instead of humans to answer questions about development is called _____ research.

8. The most rigorous method of research used to determine cause and effect relationships is the _____ method.

9. Harry Harlow's research on the effects of maternal deprivation in monkeys is an example of _____ research.

10. Scientists often speak of _____ between the organism and environment that work together to produce outcomes.

ANSWERS TO PRACTICE TEST ITEMS

MIX-AND-MATCH

1. d	2. j
3. m	4. k
5. b	6. k
7. i	8. f
9. a	10. e
11. g	12. c
13. h	

MULTIPLE CHOICE

1. c	2. d
3. c	4. a
5. b	6. a
7. b	8. d
9. b	10. a

TRUE AND FALSE

1. false	2. false
3. true	4. true
5. false	6. false
7. true	8. false
9. false	10. true

FILL-IN-THE-BLANKS

1. universal changes; individual differences; environmental influences
2. active; passive
3. environmental determinists; biological determinists
4. stages
5. applied; basic
6. independent variable; dependent variable
7. cross-species
8. experimental
9. cross-species
10. transactions

CHAPTER 2:
GENETICS AND BEHAVIOR GENETICS

CHAPTER OVERVIEW

The field of behavior genetics studies the extent to which genes affect behavior as well as the way in which they interact with environmental influences. Human cells typically have 46 chromosomes, except for sperm and egg cells, which have only 23 chromosomes. Conception occurs when a single sperm and egg unite to form a single cell composed of 46 chromosomes. Within each chromosome are thousands of smaller particles called genes, which contain information that guides and determines development. Often, genes carry different versions of a particular trait that are either dominant or recessive. The presence of dominant genes for a particular trait, e.g., brown eyes, tends to mask the influence of recessive genes, e.g., blue eyes. The term genotype refers to the underlying genetic makeup of an individual whereas phenotype refers to an individual's actual physical appearance and behavior. Due to genetic variability and environmental factors, it is possible for some people to have the same phenotype but differ in their genotype and for others to have the same genotype but differ in their phenotype.

There are numerous problems in development that are genetically based. For example, individuals born with phenylketonuria lack an enzyme that converts certain foods into harmless by-products, causing damage to the central nervous system and mental retardation. Individuals born with Down syndrome have an additional chromosome on the twenty-first pair that causes mild to severe mental retardation. Fragile-X syndrome is a condition in which the X chromosome has a constricted area that may result in breakage, causing mild to severe retardation and behavioral disorders. Klinefelter's syndrome is a condition in which males have an extra X sex chromosome, causing mild retardation and irregularities in sexual development.

Researchers have used a variety of research methods to study the role that genetics plays in determining intelligence and personality. For example, studies have revealed higher correlations in the IQ scores of monozygotic twins, who are genetically identical than in dizygotic twins, who are no more alike genetically than regular siblings. Studies also have revealed only slightly higher correlations in IQ scores of identical twins reared together than for identical twins reared apart. Finally, adoption studies have revealed that children's IQ scores tend to be more strongly correlated with their biological parents than with their adopted parents. Although these studies suggest that genes play a very important role in determining intelligence, other studies indicate that environment also exerts an important influence on intellectual development. For example, environmental influences appear to have a greater effect on academic achievement than genetic influences. Studies also indicate that genes exert a stronger influence on basic personality traits, such as shyness, than on socially-dependent traits, such as those associated with ethical and moral development. Finally, twin studies suggests that genes play an important role in the development of mental disorders, such as schizophrenia and depression but that a person's genetic susceptibility may be influenced by environmental stress and life experiences.

Researchers often refer to the concept of "reaction range" when discussing the relative influence of genetics and environment. Although genes determine the range of abilities with which individuals are born, the environment determines the potential for individuals to maximize those abilities. Some theorists believe that not only do genes determine reaction range, they also influence the type of experiences an individual has and argue that the environment has a minor impact on development. Critics argue that the genetic determinists are too vague in their definition of environment and that more research is needed before the effects of nature vs. nurture are fully understood. Finally, research that has investigated the influence of shared vs. nonshared environments of siblings has revealed that characteristics such as intelligence, personality and psychopathology are determined primarily by nonshared environments.

CHAPTER OUTLINE: Use the outline provided below by writing information related to each topic in the margins of the outline, e.g., definitions of terms and elaboration of concepts.

I. The Mechanisms of Hereditary Transmission

A. Chromosomes, genes and DNA

B. Mitosis, meiosis, and crossing-over

C. Dominant and recessive genes

D. Genotype and phenotype

II. Genetically Caused Problems in Development

A. Phenylketonuria

B. Down syndrome

C. Fragile-X syndrome

D. Klinefelter's syndrome

III. Findings of Behavior Genetics

A. Intelligence and adoption studies

B. Personality development

C. Schizophrenia

D. Depression

E. Other mental disorders

IV. Do Children Select Their Environments?

A. Reaction range

B. Passive effects of genotype

C. Evocative effects of genotype

D. Active effects of genotype

V. Why Are Siblings So Different?

A. Shared vs. nonshared environments

KEY DEFINITIONS AND TERMS: Define the following concepts and terms Try to provide an example for each word or term you have defined to help clarify its meaning.

Behavior genetics:

Genes:

Autosomes:

Sex chromosomes:

DNA:

Mitosis:

Meiosis:

Crossing-over:

Dominant gene:

Recessive gene:

Genotype :

Phenotype:

Phenylketonuria:

Down syndrome:

Fragile-X syndrome:

Klinefelters syndrome:

Polygenetic inheritance:

Monozygotic twin:

Dizygotic twin:

Schizophrenia:

Depression:

Reaction range:

Passive effects of genotype:

Evocative effects of genotype:

Active effects of genotype:

Shared environment:

Nonshared environment:

REVIEW QUESTIONS: Below are questions that relate to key concepts and information covered in your textbook. Answer the questions as thoroughly and completely as possible. Try to provide examples to support your answer and to clarify meaning.

1. Describe the processes involved in conception. How many chromosomes do eggs and sperm typically have? Why do egg and sperm cells have only half the number of chromosomes that autosomes have?

2. Describe the process of cell division known as meiosis. How and why does this process differ from mitosis? What is crossing-over and what important function does this process serve?

3. Discuss the role that sex chromosomes play in determining the sex of an individual. What combination of chromosomes results in male development and what combination results in female development? Is the birth rate higher for boys or for girls, or is the birth rate about the same?

4. What are genes and approximately how many genes are found in a single human cell? Discuss the role that dominant and recessive genes play and the processes involved in determining specific traits, such as eye color. Do people with the same phenotype necessarily have the same genotype? Is it possible for people with the same genotype to have different phenotypes? Explain.

5. Describe the disease called phenylketonuria. What genetic factor causes the development of this disease, what are some of the possible negative outcomes and how can progression of the disease be modified?

6. What is Down syndrome and what is the cause of this condition? Discuss the way in which Down syndrome affects physical and intellectual development.

7. Describe fragile-X syndrome and Klinefelter's syndrome and the role that sex chromosomes play in their development. How do each of these syndromes affect behavioral and intellectual development? According to research, how can a nurturant home environment affect the outcome of individuals born with sex-chromosome abnormalities?

8. How have researchers investigated the extent to which genetics affect intelligence? Describe the research that has compared the IQ scores of monozygotic and dizygotic twins. Do IQ scores of identical twins reared apart differ significantly from twins reared in the same environment? What do the results of these studies suggest about the relative influence of genetic versus environmental influences?

9. Describe the adoption studies that have investigated the relative effect of genetic versus environmental influences. Do adoptive children's IQ scores correlate more strongly with their biological or adoptive parents?

10. Much of the research indicates that genetic factors play an important role in determining intelligence. What two important qualifications need to be considered when interpreting the data from these studies? Discuss research that provides evidence for environmental influences on intelligence.

11. Describe the research using monozygotic and dizygotic twins that has investigated genetic influences on personality development. Do genetic factors appear to influence some behaviors more than others? Cite research to support your answer.

12. Describe the research suggesting that hereditary factors may play a role in the development of schizophrenia. What are the chances of one identical twin developing schizophrenia if the other twin has it? What is the ratio for nonidentical twins? What has research using adoption studies revealed about biological versus environmental influences?

13. Describe research that has investigated genetic influences and the development of depression as well as bipolar or manic-depressive disorders. Do studies support a genetic explanation for these diseases?

14. What is meant by the term "reaction range"? How do passive, evocative and active effects of a genotype affect a child's interaction with his or her environment? According to Scarr, how important is the environment in determining a child's development? How have critics reacted to Scarr's position?

15. Why are siblings so different? Discuss the difference between shared and nonshared environments. Do characteristics such as intelligence, personality and psychopathology appear to be under the influence of shared or nonshared environments?

16. Specify what some of the important nonshared influences are and how they might affect behavior and development.

MIX-AND-MATCH: In the left-hand column below are some key concepts or definitions. Choose the term from the column on the right that best matches each definition provided in the column on the left.

1. Small particles located on chromosomes that are carriers of a child's heredity

   a. Genotype

2. Chromosomes that are possessed equally by both males and females

   b. Reaction range

3. The pair of chromosomes that differs in males and females and determines a person's gender

   c. Mitosis

4. Critical component of genes composed of two molecular chains that are coiled around each other in a double-stranded helix

   d. Crossing-over

5. The process whereby a cell divides to reproduce itself

   e. Phenotype

6. The process whereby germ cells divide resulting in cells whose nuclei contain only half the number of chromosomes present in the parent cell

   f. Genes

7. Process that occurs during meiosis that increases the likelihood that each sperm or ovum will be unique

   g. Phenylketonuria

8. Genes that tend to dominate and determine the development of specific traits by masking the effects of other variations of the gene

   h. Autosomes

9. The underlying genetic makeup of an individual, which may or may not be manifest in outward appearance and behavior

   i. Down syndrome

10. The observed appearance and behavior of an individual, which may be the product of multiple influences, both biological and environmental

    j. Meiosis

11. Genetically based disease in which an individual lacks an enzyme needed to convert specific foods into useless by-products, which causes damage to the central nervous and mental retardation

    k. Sex chromosomes

12. A condition that occurs when an extra copy of chromosome 21 is present, causing physical and intellectual problems in development

    l. DNA

13. Term that refers to the idea that each individual's genotype sets a limit on the phenotype that can arise in individual development

    m. Dominant genes

MULTIPLE CHOICE QUESTIONS: Read the following questions and indicate your answer by marking the option that you think best answers each question.

1. The 22 pair of chromosomes that are possessed equally in males and females are called
   a. sex chromosomes.
   b. autosomes.
   c. DNA.
   d. phenotypes.

2. The process whereby a cell divides to reproduce itself is called
   a. mitosis.
   b. meiosis.
   c. crossing-over.
   d. genotyping.

3. Genes that are coded for and determine specific traits such as eye color by dominating and masking the effects of other genes are called
   a. dominant genes.
   b. recessive genes.
   c. genotypes.
   d. phenotypes.

4. The disease in which an individual lacks the enzyme needed to convert some foods into harmless by-products causing CNS damage and mental retardation is
   a. Down syndrome.
   b. Klinefelter's syndrome.
   c. fragile-X syndrome.
   d. phenylketonuria.

5. Studies that have studied the effect of genetic influences on intelligence have revealed that
   a. correlations of IQ scores are higher among monozygotic twins than dizygotic twins.
   b. correlations of IQ scores are higher among dizygotic twins than monozygotic.
   c. correlations of IQ scores are among monozygotic twins reared apart are extremely low.
   d. genetic factors do not appear to significantly affect intelligence.

6. Which of the following statements best summarizes the known effects that genetic factors have on the development of personality?
   a. Genetic factors are strongest for basic temperamental characteristics e.g., shyness.
   b. Genetic factors appear to be strongest for traits that govern ethical and social values.
   c. Genetic factors do not appear to be significantly related to personality in any way.
   d. It is not possible to scientifically assess the role that genetics plays in personality.

7. Research that has investigated the genetic influences on schizophrenia has revealed that
   a. if one identical twin has it, chances are about one in two that the other will develop it.
   b. the ratio among nonidentical twins is less than one in ten.
   c. there are no apparent genetic influences in the development of schizophrenia.
   d. both "a" and "b" are correct.

8. Males who are born with an additional X chromosome have the condition known as
   a. fragile-X syndrome.
   b. Down syndrome.
   c. Klinefelter's syndrome.
   d. phenylketonuria.

9. Fragile-X syndrome is caused by
   a. nutritional influences and diet.
   b. exposure to alcohol during the prenatal period that impairs fetal development.
   c. environmental influences after an individual is born.
   d. a partial breakage of the X chromosome that may result in retardation.

10. The pairing of two recessive genes will lead to the development of
    a. brown eyes.
    b. blue eyes.
    c. Down syndrome.
    d. a chromosomal abnormality.

TRUE AND FALSE QUESTIONS: Read the following statements and indicate whether you think each statement is true or false.

1. The term genotype refers to the observable traits and behaviors of an individual.

2. Down syndrome can be avoided totally through medications and by modifying a child's diet.

3. A sperm and an egg each contains 23 chromosomes.

4. The process that results in the production of cells whose nuclei contain only half the number of chromosomes present in the parent cell is called meiosis.

5. Crossing-over increases the likelihood that two people in the same family will be unique.

6. Studies on twins strongly suggest that genetic factors have little effect on the development of intelligence.

7. Klinefelter's syndrome is a chromosomal abnormality that affects males and females equally.

8. Genetic factors are most likely to influence basic personality traits such as shyness.

9. Schizophrenia is more prevalent in fraternal twins than in identical twins.

10. The IQ scores of adopted children tend to be more highly correlated with children's adoptive parents than with their biological parents.

FILL-IN-THE-BLANKS: Read the following sentences and write the missing word or words in the space provided.

1. The field of _____ studies the extent to which genes affect behavior as well as the way in which they interact with environmental influences.

2. Genes that determine brown eyes are _____ and genes that determine blue eyes are _____.

3. Chromosomes that are shared equally by males and females are called _____ and the twenty-third pair of chromosomes, which differs for males and females, are the _____ chromosomes.

4. The term _____ refers to the underlying genetic makeup of an individual whereas _____ refers to an individual's actual physical appearance and behavior.

5. Males born with an extra X chromosome which may cause mental retardation and irregularities in their sexual development have the disorder known as _____.

6. The condition in which an X chromosome has a constricted area near the tip that may result in breakage and cause mild to severe retardation and behavioral disorders is called _____.

7. The term _____ refers to the idea that each individual's genotype sets a limit on the phenotype that can arise in individual development.

8. Monozygotic twins are twins who are _____ identical.

9. The term _____ refers to characteristics which may be due to the presence of a number of genes.

10. There are approximately _____ genes in a single human cell.

ANSWERS TO PRACTICE TEST ITEMS

MIX-AND-MATCH

1. f	2. h
3. k	4. l
5. c	6. j
7. d	8. m
9. a	10. e
11. g	12. i
13. b	

MULTIPLE CHOICE

1. b	2. a
3. a	4. d
5. a	6. a
7. d	8. c
9. d	10. b

TRUE AND FALSE

1. false	2. false
3. true	4. true
5. true	6. false
7. false	8. true
9. false	10. false

FILL-IN-THE-BLANKS

1. behavior genetics
2. dominant; recessive
3. autosomes; sex chromosomes
4. genotype; phenotype
5. Klinefelter's syndrome
6. fragile-X syndrome
7. reaction range
8. genetically
9. polygenetic inheritance
10. one million

Prenatal development can be divided into three stages. The germinal period begins at the time of conception and ends when the fertilized egg implants on the uterine wall. The fertilized egg, called a zygote, travels through the Fallopian tube to the uterus, where it implants and continues to grow and develop. Implantation marks the beginning of the embryonic period and the zygote is now called an embryo. During this period structures such as the amniotic sac, umbilical cord and placenta develop and other structures, such as the brain and heart, become more clearly differentiated. During the fetal period, which lasts from the end of the second month until birth, various systems of the body begin to function. Fetal movement can be detected by the sixteenth week, but it is not until the twenty-eighth week that the fetus reaches the age of viability. After the twenty-eighth week there is a rapid increase in the fetus's weight and height and by the end of the ninth month, the average baby weighs approximately 7 pounds and is 20 to 21 inches in length.

Several factors can adversely affect prenatal development. Women over the age of 40 are at an increased risk for having a baby with chromosomal abnormalities. Poor prenatal nutrition has been linked with low infant birth weight, impaired cognitive development and higher infant mortality rates. Drinking alcohol during pregnancy can retard growth and also is associated with mental retardation, physical deformities and heart disease. Nicotine can retard fetal growth and increases the risk of miscarriage and premature birth. Cocaine use during pregnancy has been associated with premature birth, lower birth weight, smaller head circumference, irregular sleep problems, and abnormal reflexes. Exposure to radiation has been linked to fetal death, brain damage, shorter life span, and risk for certain cancers. Viral diseases, such as Rubella, may result in fetal abnormalities and mental retardation. Exposure to genital herpes can cause congenital abnormalities and neurological damage. The AIDS virus can pass from the infected mother prenatally, during birth, and through breastfeeding. The bacteria that cause syphilis can pass through the placenta by the fourth or fifth month of pregnancy and infect the developing fetus. Rh incompatibility can cause mild to severe problems in development. Maternal stress can affect the circulatory system of the fetus and has been linked with premature birth, low birth weight, hyperactivity and irritability. Finally, research has established a link between paternal age and an increase in genetic abnormalities in offspring.

Several medical procedures currently are used to detect fetal abnormalities. Amniocentesis is a procedure conducted between the sixteenth and eighteenth weeks of pregnancy, whereby a needle is inserted into the amniotic sac in order to extract a small amount of fluid. Fetal cells contained in the fluid are then analyzed for the presence of over 75 genetically-based diseases. Chorionic villi sampling involves extracting a sample of cells from the placenta which then are analyzed for genetically based disorders, but it may increase a woman's chance of miscarriage. Ultrasound is a procedure whereby sound waves produce an image of the developing fetus, allowing physicians to detect structural abnormalities as well as the sex of the baby.

Labor can be divided into three stages. In the first stage, the cervix thins and uterine contractions cause it to dilate fully . Delivery occurs during the second stage of labor when the mother actively pushes the baby out through the birth canal. The third stage of labor involves delivery of the placenta. If complications during labor pose a risk to the mother or the baby, a Cesarean section may be performed in which the baby is surgically removed from the uterus. Women have the option of taking drugs during labor. However, drugs may interfere with labor and their effects must be monitored carefully by the physician. Postnatal problems, such as anoxia, can result in long-term defects in motor development, such as cerebral palsy. Finally, premature infants are at risk for numerous medical problems, such as respiratory distress syndrome, intracranial hemorrhaging and death and must be carefully monitored.

CHAPTER OUTLINE: Use the outline provided below by writing information related to each topic in the margins of the outline, e.g., definitions of terms and elaboration of concepts.

I. Stages of Prenatal Development

A.. *The germinal period*

B. *The embryonic period*

C. *The fetal period*

II. Prenatal Environment Influences

A. *Age of the mother*

B. *Maternal nutrition*

C. *Drugs and radiation*

III. Maternal Diseases and Disorders

A. *The Rh factor*

B. *Maternal stress*

C. *Paternal effects*

IV. Prenatal Testing

A. *Chorionic villi sampling*

B. *Amniocentesis*

C. *Ultrasound scans*

V. The Birth Process

A. *Vaginal delivery*

B. *Stages of labor*

C. *Cesarean section*

D. *Drugs taken during labor and delivery*

E *Anoxia and other complications*

F. *Prematurity*

KEY DEFINITIONS AND TERMS: Define the following concepts and terms Try to provide an example for each word or term you have defined to help clarify its meaning.

Germinal period:

Embryonic stage:

Fetal stage:

Zygote:

Trophoblast:

Ectoderm:

Mesoderm:

Endoderm:

Chorion:

Amnion:

Amniotic fluid:

Umbilical cord:

Placenta:

Placental barrier:

Viability:

Teratogens:

Fetal alcohol syndrome:

Rh Factor:

Chorionic villi sampling:

Amniocentesis:

Ultrasound:

Effacement:

Dilation:

First stage of labor:

Second stage of labor:

Third stage of labor:

Transition:

Cesarean section:

Epidural:

Anoxia:

Respiratory Distress Syndrome:

Intracranial hemorrhage:

REVIEW QUESTIONS: Below are questions that relate to key concepts and information covered in your textbook. Answer the questions as thoroughly and completely as possible. Try to provide examples to support your answer and to clarify meaning.

1. Describe the processes involved in conception. When does a zygote begin to subdivide? On average, how long does it take an ovum to travel from the Fallopian tube to the uterus?

2. Describe the changes that occur during the germinal stage of prenatal development. Into what structures do the inner and outer portions of the trophoblast develop? When does the germinal stage begin and end?

3. Describe the developmental changes that occur during the embryonic stage. Into what structures do the ectoderm, mesoderm and endoderm of the inner cells develop? What develops from the outer layers of cells? What other changes in development take place? When does the embryonic stage begin and end?

4. What important functions do the umbilical cord, placenta and placental barrier serve in prenatal growth and development? What are some of the substances that are known to pass through the placenta and affect fetal development?

5. Describe the changes that occur during the fetal stage of development. What important systems develop during this period and when do they develop? When is the age of viability?

6. Discuss the effects that maternal age can have on fertility and on the health of both the mother and developing baby. What are the most favorable ages for childbearing?

7. Discuss the role that nutrition plays in prenatal development and growth. What aspects of diet are especially important in the first few weeks of pregnancy? What are some of the developmental problems that are associated with babies born to mothers with nutritionally deficient diets?

8. Discuss the harmful effects on prenatal development that are associated with alcohol. What is "fetal alcohol syndrome," and what are the physical and cognitive problems in development that are caused by alcohol consumption during pregnancy?

9. Discuss the harmful effects on prenatal development that are associated with the following: nicotine, caffeine, cocaine and radiation. Be specific.

10. Discuss the known effects that the following diseases and disorders during pregnancy can have on fetal development: Rubella, genital herpes, AIDS, syphilis, and toxemia.

11. What is the Rh Factor and how can Rh incompatibility affect fetal development? How is Rh compatibility treated and prevented?

12. How can a mother's emotional state affect the developing fetus? Discuss the known effects that maternal stress can have on fetal development.

13. What is known about the effect that paternal influences can have on a baby's risk of having genetic disorders? In what other nongenetic ways can factors cause problems in fetal development?

14. Describe the following testing procedures, when they are usually performed, and what diagnostic information they provide about the developing fetus: chorionic villi sampling, amniocentesis and ultrasound scan.

15. Describe the three stages of labor and what occurs during each stage. What is a Cesarean section and under what conditions might a Cesarean section be performed?

16. What is anoxia and what are some of the complications that might result from anoxia in a newborn?

17. Discuss some of the problems associated with infants who are born prematurely. How can the age of the premature infant, its birth weight, and the type of postnatal care it receives influence the long-term effects on development? When is an infant considered to be premature?

MIX-AND-MATCH: In the left-hand column below are some key concepts or definitions. Choose the term from the column on the right that best matches each definition provided in the column on the left.

1. Period of prenatal development that lasts from conception until implantation

   a. Teratogens

2. Period of prenatal development that extends from the second to the eighth week

   b. Umbilical cord

3. Period of prenatal development that extends from the eight week of pregnancy to delivery

   c. Fetal alcohol syndrome

4. Term that refers to a fertilized egg prior to implantation

   d. Ultrasound scan

5. The "lifeline" through which blood is passed between the embryo and placenta

   e. Effacement

6. Substances taken during pregnancy that can cause birth defects

   f. Embryonic period

7. Term used to describe defects in fetal development that are due to excessive alcohol consumption during pregnancy

   g. Third stage of labor

8. Diagnostic procedure in which a fetal image is produce by way of sound waves

   h. Fetal period

9. Term used to describe the thinning of the cervix that occurs during the first stage of labor

   i. Amniocentesis

10. Stage of labor during which the cervix becomes fully effaced and dilated

    j. Germinal period

11. Stage of labor during which delivery of the baby occurs

    k. Second stage of labor

12. Stage of labor during which delivery of the placenta occurs

    l. Chorion villi sampling

13. Type of delivery in which the baby is surgically removed from the uterus

    m. Zygote

14. Diagnostic procedure performed between the 16th and 18th weeks of pregnancy in which a needle is inserted through the abdominal wall and amniotic fluid is extracted

    n. First stage of labor

15. Procedure in which cells are gathered from the placenta either through a catheter that is inserted in the cervix or a needle inserted in the abdomen

    o. Cesarean section

46

MULTIPLE CHOICE QUESTIONS: Read the following questions and indicate your answer by marking the option that you think best answers each question.

1. Research that has investigated paternal effects on fetal development has revealed that
   a. the risk of genetic disorders increases with paternal age.
   b. the risk of genetic disorders decreases with paternal age.
   c. paternal age is unrelated to risk of genetic disorders.
   d. semen cannot affect development because it cannot pass viruses or diseases to the fetus.

2. Research that has investigated the effects of maternal stress has revealed that
   a. stress can cause a release of hormones that changes the fetus's circulatory system.
   b. the placental barrier protects the fetus from any harmful effects of maternal stress.
   c. infants are more likely to be premature and have low birth weight.
   d. both "a" and "c" are correct.

3. Research that has investigated the effect of maternal age has revealed that
   a. more complications and risks to mother and baby occur among women over 40.
   b. more complications and risks to mother and baby occur among teenage girls.
   c. the fewest complications and risks to mother and baby occur among teenage girls.
   d. both "a" and "b" are correct.

4. The most favorable years for childbearing are between ages
   a. 15-19.
   b. 20-35.
   c. 30-40.
   d. 35-45.

5. Which of the following conditions can result from anoxia in a newborn?
   a. Down syndrome
   b. Tay-Sachs disease
   c. cerebral palsy
   d. all of the above

6. Which of the following problems in development affects infants born with fetal alcohol syndrome?
   a. mental retardation
   b. premature birth
   c. congenital heart disease
   d. all of the above

7. The medical procedure that involves gathering cells from the placenta either through a catheter inserted into the cervix or a needle inserted in the abdomen is called
   a. amniocentesis.
   b. chorionic villi sampling.
   c. an ultrasound scan.
   d. placental extraction.

8. On average, the fertilized egg will reach the uterus in
   a. 24 hours.
   b. one to two days.
   c. three to seven days.
   d. two to three weeks.

9. The structure through which arteries pass blood between the embryo and placenta and which is sometimes referred to as the baby's "lifeline" is called the
   a. embryonic membrane.
   b. umbilical cord.
   c. chorion.
   d. placental tube.

10. Babies born to mothers with nutritionally deficient diets are at greater risk for
   a. spina bifida.
   b. impaired brain development.
   c. impaired cognitive development.
   d. all of the above.

TRUE AND FALSE QUESTIONS: Read the following statements and indicate whether you think each statement is true or false.

1. Infertility and the risk of having a baby with chromosomal abnormalities increase with the age of the mother.

2. The risk of having a baby with chromosomal abnormalities does not appear to increase with the age of the father.

3. The teen years are considered to be the most favorable for childbearing.

4. Research indicates that drinking small to moderate amounts of alcohol during pregnancy does not significantly affect fetal development.

5. Children of mothers who smoke cigarettes during their pregnancy tend to have impulsive behavior, poor attention and poor memory.

6. The negative consequences of Rh incompatibility can be prevented by giving the mother a vaccine that destroys the baby's Rh-positive cells.

7. Delivery of the baby occurs during the third stage of labor.

8. Dilation and effacement of the cervix occur during the second stage of labor.

9. Anoxia in a newborn can be the cause of a variety of motor defects including cerebral palsy.

10. Premature infants are those born earlier than the thirty-eighth week and weighing less than five pounds.

FILL-IN-THE-BLANKS: Read the following sentences and write the missing word or words in the space provided.

1. Semipermeable membranes that separate the mother's and fetus's bloodstreams and function as extremely fine screens are referred to as the _____.

2. The period that lasts from the time of implantation to the end of the second month is called the _____.

3. Substances taken during pregnancy that can cause birth defects in the developing fetus are called _____.

4. Drinking alcohol during pregnancy can cause a baby to be born with a condition called _____.

5. The negative consequences of Rh compatibility can be prevented by giving the mother a _____ that destroys the baby's Rh-positive blood cells.

6. The term _____ refers to the thinning of the cervix in the first stage of labor, and the term _____ refers to the opening and enlargement of the cervix.

7. The delivery of the baby occurs during the _____ stage of labor.

8. An _____ is a medical procedure in which painkillers are injected into the mother's spinal cord during labor.

9. Both hemorrhaging and failure to breathe affect the supply of oxygen to the nerve cells of the brain and produce a state called _____.

10. Premature infants are those born earlier than the _____ week of gestation and weighing less than _____ pounds.

MIX-AND-MATCH

1.	j	2.	f
3.	h	4.	m
5.	b	6.	a
7.	c	8.	d
9.	e	10.	n
11.	k	12.	g
13.	o	14.	l
15.	l		

MULTIPLE CHOICE

1.	a	2.	d
3.	d	4.	b
5.	c	6.	d
7.	b	8.	c
9.	b	10.	d

TRUE AND FALSE

1.	true	2.	false
3.	false	4.	false
5.	true	6.	true
7.	false	8.	false
9.	true	10.	true

MIX-AND-MATCH

1. placental barrier
2. germinal period
3. teratogens
4. fetal alcohol syndrome
5. vaccine
6. effacement; dilation
7. second
8. epidural
9. anoxia
10. thirty-eighth; five

CHAPTER OVERVIEW

Several theories that differ somewhat in their assumptions and beliefs about infant development have been proposed. Freud believed that the infant's stimulation of the oral region during the first year of life served as an important outlet for the energy of the libido. Erikson proposed that establishing trust with the caregiver was the most critical stage of development in the infant's first year of life. Bowlby's theory proposed that in the first few years of life, strong emotional bonds develop between infants and their caregiver that serve an important adaptive function. Piaget's theory focused on the sensory and motor skills that develop in the first year of life and on the ability of infants to manipulate objects in their environment. Each theory has generated valuable research and contributed to a richer understanding of infant development.

Infants undergo rapid development in the first year of life but are unable to engage in various cognitive and motor skills until their brain and body have sufficiently developed, a process called maturation. Critical periods of development for some skills appear to be determined by maturational processes and influenced by experience. Infants are born with a set of inherited reflexes, many of which have important adaptive functions. Most reflexes gradually will end as the cerebral cortex matures and infants develop motor skills. During the first year, motor skills progress from sitting to crawling, standing, and walking. Sleep patterns also change during infancy, with the total amount of sleep decreasing from 18 to 12 hours a day by age two, and REM sleep decreasing from about 50 percent in the newborn to 20 percent by adulthood.

Although almost all of the neurons an individual will ever have are in place by the seventh month of prenatal development, numerous postnatal changes occur. Subtractive events appear to have the function of selectively eliminating an overabundance of nerve cells and connections. Additive events are processes that improve the efficiency of the nervous system, such as the formation of axons, myelination and synaptogenesis. In addition to maturational processes, environmental influences and experience also appear to play an important role in the development of the neural system during critical periods of development.

Learning and conditioning processes help infants adapt to their environment. Classical conditioning occurs when a previously neutral stimulus acquires the capacity to evoke a response by way of its repeated association with a stimulus that normally evokes the response. It can occur within the first few hours after birth and does not appear to be dependent on memory processes. Instrumental conditioning occurs when a behavior is followed by a successful outcome, increasing the likelihood that the behavior will occur again. Instrumental conditioning has been useful in teaching retarded children basic skills and reducing specific fears in children.

Habituation-dishabituation, visual preference and high-amplitude sucking are methods that determine an infant's interest in a particular stimulus and are useful in the assessment of various perceptual skills. For example, studies using these methods have found that visual acuity and depth perception dramatically improve in the first few months of life and that infants are able to discriminate color categories and complex perceptual patterns. Studies also reveal that infants hear quite well, are capable of auditory localization, and are sensitive to temperature, taste and smell. Finally, studies indicate that babies are capable of cross-modal perception, the ability to anticipate one sense through their experience with another sense. Determining normal ranges of abilities has been extremely useful in neonatal assessment and identifying potential problems in development. Not all potential medical problems can be predicted, however. Although research has identified risk factors that are associated with sudden infant death syndrome, such as premature birth and low birth weight, doctors cannot predict precisely which babies are at risk.

CHAPTER OUTLINE: Use the outline provided below by writing information related to each topic in the margins of the outline, e.g., definitions of terms and elaboration of concepts.

I. Theories and Assumptions:

A. Freud's theory

B. Erikson's theory

C. Bowlby's theory

D. Piaget's theory

II. Physical Development

A. Physical growth

B. Maturation

C. Reflexes

D. Motor development

E. Sleep

F. Maturation of the brain

III. Learning and Conditioning

A. Classical conditioning

B. Instrumental learning

IV. Perceptual Development

A. Vision

B. Hearing

C. Touch, taste and smell

D. Cross-modal perception

V. Applications

A. Neonatal assessment

B. Sudden infant death syndrome

KEY DEFINITIONS AND TERMS: Define the following concepts and terms Try to provide an example for each word or term you have defined to help clarify its meaning.

Oral stage:

Stage of trust:

Attachment:

Sensorimotor period:

Maturation:

Critical periods:

Rooting reflex:

Moro reflex:

REM sleep:

Neurons:

Dendrites :

Axons:

Synapse:

Myelination:

Synaptogenesis:

Classical conditioning:

Instrumental conditioning:

Primary reinforcer:

Secondary reinforcer:

Habituation-dishabituation:

Visual preference techniques:

High-amplitude sucking:

Stereopsis:

Auditory localization:

Cross-modal perception:

Neonatal Behavior Assessment Scale:

Sudden Infant Death Syndrome:

REVIEW QUESTIONS: Below are questions that relate to key concepts and information covered in your textbook. Answer the questions as thoroughly and completely as possible. Try to provide examples to support your answer and to clarify meaning.

1. Describe the views of the following theorists: Sigmund Freud, Erik Erikson, John Bowlby and Jean Piaget. On what aspect of infant development did each of these theorists focus and in what way did their theories reflect the larger cultural context in which they were developed?

2. Describe some of the physical growth and changes that occur in the first year of life. How is an infant's growth rate affected by socioeconomic factors?

3. What is meant by the term "maturation"? Why is it not possible to teach a five-month-old to speak and understand language? Discuss the importance of experience during "critical periods" of development.

4. Describe the Moro reflex and the rooting reflex. Why are infants born with so many reflexes? Do all reflexes serve an adaptive purpose? Why or why not? In what order do the various motor skills develop? Discuss the role of experience in determining when motor skills develop. What are some of the socioemotional consequences of motor development?

5. What are the six states of infant sleep and which sleep state is optimal for learning and interacting with others? How do sleep patterns change as infants grow and mature? How do cultures differ in how they manage infant sleep?

6. What are the components of neurons, how do neurons transmit information and by what age are most neurons in place? What function do "subtractive events" in the nervous system serve? What are the three "additive events" that occur in the nervous system and what functions do they serve?

7. What is classical conditioning and what is the earliest age that an infant can be classically conditioned? Does classical conditioning appear to be dependent on memory processes? Support your answer by citing relevant studies.

8. What is instrumental conditioning and how soon can infants be instrumentally conditioned? Are infants able to discriminate cues in the environment that signal when and what behaviors will be reinforced? Can infants learn what response will be reinforced, based on internally coded rules? Cite relevant studies to support your answer.

9.   Describe the following methods that are used in the study of perceptual development in infants: habituation-dishabituation, visual preference and high-amplitude techniques. How can each of these methods allow researchers to draw conclusions about perceptual abilities?

10. Describe the visual abilities and tendencies of infants and the methods that are used to test them. How are the visual acuity and depth perception of infants tested? Do infants appear to like or dislike stimuli that provide visual variety and contrast? Do infants perceive colors as belonging to discrete categories? Are they able to process complex perceptual patterns?

11. Describe the hearing abilities of infants. How soon are infants able to remember voices? What is auditory localization and when do infants have this hearing ability? How and why does this ability change over time?

12. Discuss the infant's sensitivity to temperature, touch, taste and smell. What is cross-modal perception and how has this ability been tested in infants?

13. Describe some of the tests that have been devised to assess newborns, including the Neonatal Behavior Assessment Scale. How can the NBSA help parents to be more responsive to their babies and more knowledgeable about them later?

14. What is sudden infant death syndrome and at what age is it most likely to occur? Discuss what is known about the circumstances of SIDS and the risk factors that are associated with it. Can pediatricians predict in any precise way which babies are at risk? At present, is there a known cause of SIDS?

MIX-AND-MATCH: In the left-hand column below are some key concepts or definitions. Choose the term from the column on the right that best matches each definition provided in the column on the left.

1. Theorist who believed that stimulation of the mouth, lips and tongue during infancy served as an outlet for the energy of the libido

2. Theorist who believed the most crucial task in the first year was the establishment of trust between the infant and caregiver

3. Theorist who emphasized the importance of emotional bonding and attachment between the the infant and caregiver

4. Theorist who focused on the development of sensory and motor skills and the active manipulation of objects in the first year of life

5. The universal sequences of biological events that occur in the body and the brain

6. Periods during which particular experiences are crucial for normal development

7. Response whereby babies will turn their head in the direction of a stroke to the cheek, open their their mouth and try to suck

8. Process of learning whereby a particular event that occurs frequently in conjunction with another event that automatically produces a response also acquires the ability to evoke that response

9. Process of learning whereby a behavior is followed by a successful outcome that reinforces the behavior, thereby increasing the probability that it will occur again

10. Any reinforcing event that reduces a biological drive

11. Any objects or people that are present when a biological drive is reduced that then acquires reinforcing value

12. The ability to recognize the direction from which which a sound originates

13. The ability to detect a similarity between two events when the events originate in different sense modalities

a. Classical conditioning

b. Secondary reinforcers

c. Critical periods

d. Instrumental conditioning

e. Freud

f. Maturation

g. Primary reinforcer

h. Erikson

i. Cross-modal perception

j. Auditory localization

k. Piaget

l. Bowlby

m. Rooting reflex

MULTIPLE CHOICE QUESTIONS: Read the following questions and indicate your answer by marking the option that you think best answers each question.

1. The theorist who focused on the development of sensory and motor skills and the infant's ability to manipulate objects in the environment was
    a. Jean Piaget.
    b. Sigmund Freud.
    c. John Bowlby.
    d. Erik Erikson.

2. The startle response, in which an infant's arms spread wide and then slowly come together at the midline as the legs are also brought up, is called the
    a. Babinski reflex.
    b. Moro reflex.
    c. rooting reflex.
    d. withdrawal reflex.

3. Research investigating the sleep pattern of infants has revealed that
    a. the total amount of time spent sleeping decreases as infants grow older.
    b. the total amount of time spent sleeping increases as infants grow older.
    c. the total amount of REM sleep increases as infants grow older.
    d. the infant sleep cycle is very similar to the night-day cycle of most adults.

4. Which of the following would <u>not</u> be an additive event that occurs during postnatal neural development?
    a. formation of connections among the major brain regions through the growth of axons.
    b. the process called myelination.
    c. an increase in the number of synapses among neurons in the cortex.
    d. the selective elimination of nerve cells and connections.

5. Research on classical conditioning and learning has revealed that
    a. it is an effective way to train animals but does not work on humans.
    b. newborns are not capable of learning a classically conditioned response.
    c. classical conditioning is dependent on explicit memory of the pairings or events.
    d. a newborn only two hours old is able to learn a classically conditioned response.

6. The decreased interest or boredom in an infant that accompanies the repeated presentation of a stimulus is called
    a. habituation.
    b. dishabituation.
    c. discrimination.
    d. stereopsis.

7. Six-month-old Elizabeth is given a nubby nipple to suck on but is unable to see it. Later when she is shown both a smooth and nubby nipple, she looks longer at the nipple she explored with her tongue. Which of the following abilities is she demonstrating?
    a. auditory localization.
    b. dishabituation.
    c. cross-modal perception.
    d. stereopsis.

8. Which of the following statements regarding the visual abilities of infants is false?
   a. Infants prefer stimuli that have a great deal of visual variety.
   b. Visual acuity increases dramatically in the first months of life.
   c. Infants are able to use stereopsis generally between the ages of 15 and 20 weeks.
   d. Infants are unable to perceive colors as belonging to discrete categories.

9. Research on the sensory abilities of infants has revealed that
   a. newborns are unable to detect changes in temperature.
   b. newborns appear to be sensitive to taste but not to smell.
   c. newborns appear to be sensitive to smell but not to taste.
   d. massage or tactile stimulation of premature infants improves their growth.

10. Research on sudden infant death syndrome has revealed that
   a. it tends to be more common in girls than in boys.
   b. it appears to be more common in babies who are put to sleep on their stomachs.
   c. it is not significantly related to premature birth or birth weight.
   d. both "a" and "c" are true.

TRUE AND FALSE QUESTIONS: Read the following statements and indicate whether you think each statement is true or false.

1. Significant increases in the length and weight of an infant do not usually begin until after the first year of life.

2. Maturational processes guarantee that specific functions, such as language, will develop regardless of environmental circumstances.

3. All of the reflexes that are observed in newborns and infants serve important adaptive functions that allow them to adjust to their environment.

4. Axon growth, myelination and synaptogenesis are all examples of postnatal additive events that take place in the nervous system.

5. Research has revealed that newborns who are only two hours old are able to learn a classically conditioned response.

6. Unlike adults, infants do not appear to be able to perceive colors as belonging to discrete categories.

7. Infants as young as three days old appear to be capable of distinguishing their mother's voice from the voice of a stranger.

8. Psychologists have found that visual acuity does not increase significantly until after the first year.

9. Research indicates that overall, the perceptual abilities of infants, such as hearing and vision, are extremely limited.

10. The incidence of SIDS deaths appears to be greater for infants put to sleep on their backs than for those put to sleep on their stomachs.

FILL-IN-THE-BLANKS: Read the following sentences and write the missing word or words in the space provided.

1. The term _____ refers to universal sequences of biological events occurring in the body and brain.

2. For some psychological functions, it appears that there are periods in early life sometimes called _____, during which particular experiences are crucial for normal development.

3. The projections on the neuron that receive impulses from other cells are called _____, and the long projections that carry outgoing messages are called _____.

4. Postnatal changes in the nervous system that involve the selective elimination of nerve cells and connections are referred to as _____, and processes such as myelination and synaptogenesis are referred to as _____.

5. Reinforcing events that reduce a biological drive, such as hunger or thirst, are called _____ and objects or people that are present when the biological drive is reduced that acquire reinforcing value are called _____.

6. The term that describes the decreased interest or boredom in an infant that accompanies the repeated presentation of a stimulus is called _____, and the recovery of interest in response to the new event is called _____.

7. The ability of the brain to use information derived from the fact that the right and left eyes generate two slightly different images of an object is called _____.

8. The ability of infants to detect a similarity between two events when the events originate in different sense modalities is referred to as _____.

9. Learning that occurs when two events are repeatedly paired together to form new associations is called _____, and the process of learning that occurs when behavior is followed by a successful outcome is called _____.

10. The incidence of SIDS death is greater for infants who are put to sleep on their _____ and whose mothers have _____ or used _____.

ANSWERS TO PRACTICE TEST ITEMS

MIX-AND-MATCH

1.	e	2.	h
3.	l	4.	k
5.	f	6.	c
7.	m	8.	a
9.	d	10.	g
11.	b	12.	j
13.	i		

MULTIPLE CHOICE

1.	a	2.	b
3.	a	4.	d
5.	d	6.	a
7.	c	8.	d
9.	d	10.	b

TRUE AND FALSE

1.	false	2.	false
3.	false	4.	true
5.	true	6.	false
7.	true	8.	false
9.	false	10.	false

FILL-IN-THE-BLANKS

1. maturation
2. critical periods
3. dendrites; axons
4. subtractive events; additive events
5. primary reinforcers; secondary reinforcers
6. habituation; dishabituation
7. stereopsis
8. cross-modal perception
9. classical conditioning; instrumental conditioning
10. stomach; smoked cigarettes; cocaine

CHAPTER 5:
COGNITIVE DEVELOPMENT IN INFANCY

CHAPTER OVERVIEW

One of the most influential theories in the field of child development is Piaget's theory of cognitive development. Piaget's theory became prominent in the 1960s when behaviorism dominated psychology and the bulk of research focused on the effect of environmental influences on learning and development. Piaget challenged learning theory's view that children play a passive role in their development, arguing that development is the product of both maturation and experience. A major tenet of Piaget's theory is that humans are naturally curious and actively explore and interact with their environment. Piaget also proposed that humans have an inherent ability to organize their experience into cognitive "structures," or mental representations that enable them to understand and adapt to their environment. According to Piaget, learning is an ongoing process in which individuals assimilate new information into existing structures and then reorganize existing cognitive structures in order to accommodate the information.

Piaget proposed that individuals go through four stages of cognitive development and that each stage constitutes a new and fundamentally different way in which humans process and organize their experience and understanding of the world. Piaget referred to the first 18 months as the "sensorimotor period." During this period, infants acquire information about the world primarily through interactions with their environment. Early in infancy, babies start to repeat specific actions that begin initially as reflexes. By the age of six months, infants acquire the ability to coordinate specific actions into behavioral "schemes" and are able to systematically manipulate objects in their environment. Toward the end of the first year, they are able to coordinate behavioral schemes in order to reach a specific goal, and by the end of the sensorimotor period they are able to use internal mental representations to invent new schemes.

Although Piaget revolutionized the field of child development, some of his theory and research have been challenged. For example, Piaget believed that infants are not able to understand the concept of object permanence until approximately 18 months. However, more current research reveals that infants may acquire a concept of object permanence as early as five months old. Studies also indicate that memory processes begin earlier than Piaget proposed. Research has revealed that recognition memory and memory for conditioned responses are well developed by the age of three months and that infants have the capacity for recall memory after six or eight months. Thus, current research reveals that the capacity to recognize and recall information begins early in infancy and suggests that infants are capable of cognitive processes earlier than proposed by Piaget.

Researchers also have been interested in determining the age at which infants are capable of categorization. Studies indicate that babies between the ages of two and three months show greater interest in things and events that are somewhat different from events of the past, indicating that they are capable of creating categories. Studies also reveal that infants as young as three months old show less interest in prototypical images, even though they may have never seen them before, and notice attributes that correlate as early as 10 months. Research also indicates that by the age of one year, babies are more likely to categorize objects taxonomically than to categorize based on thematic relations. Finally, studies reveal that infants see the world as organized into objects before they are actually capable of grasping and manipulating objects.

Previous measures of infant intelligence, e.g., the Bayley Scale of Infant Intelligence, have not proved to be reliable predictors of adult intelligence. However, newer testing procedures which have examined individual differences in habituation and recognition memory, reveal that both procedures successfully predict IQ scores in childhood several years later.

CHAPTER OUTLINE: Use the outline provided below by writing information related to each topic in the margins of the outline, e.g., definitions of terms and elaboration of concepts.

I. **Piaget's Theory of Cognitive Development**

    A. *Major themes*

    B. *Maturation and experience*

    C. *The active, constructive child*

    D. *Organization and adaptation*

    E. *Cognitive structures*

    fF *Assimilation and accommodation*

II. **Developmental Stages**

    A. *The sensorimotor period*

    B. *The preoperational stage*

    C. *Concrete operations*

    D. *Formal operations*

III. **The Sensorimotor Period**

    A. *Sensorimotor schemes*

    B. *Problem solving*

    C. *Object permanence*

IV. **New Evidence on Infant Cognition**

    A. *Object permanence*

    B. *Memory and representation*

    C. *Categories*

    D. *Perception of objects*

V. **Assessing Infant Intelligence**

    A. *Newer testing procedures*

KEY DEFINITIONS AND TERMS: Define the following concepts and terms Try to provide an example for each word or term you have defined to help clarify its meaning.

Competence vs. performance:

Cognitive Structures:

Operations:

Assimilation:

Accommodation:

Disequilibrium:

Equilibrium:

Sensorimotor stage:

Preoperational stage:

Concrete operational stage:

Formal operational stage:

Sensorimotor scheme:

Primary circular reactions:

Secondary circular reactions:

Tertiary circular reactions:

Object permanence:

Recognition memory:

Recall memory:

Delayed imitation:

Category:

Discrepant events:

Prototype formation:

Bayley Scale of Infant Development:

REVIEW QUESTIONS: Below are questions that relate to key concepts and information covered in your textbook. Answer the questions as thoroughly and completely as possible. Try to provide examples to support your answer and to clarify meaning.

1. Discuss the way in which developmental psychologists conduct research that allows them to make inferences about thought from behavior. Why is it important for researchers to make the distinction between competence and performance?

2. Describe the major themes of Piaget's theory of development. How did Piaget's theory differ from the behavioral view of child development? According to Piaget, what are the two basic principles guiding human development?

3. Describe the four stages of development proposed by Piaget. According to Piaget, how do cognitive abilities differ in each of these stages?

4. Describe the sensorimotor period and some of the changes that occur during this stage of development. Include examples of primary, secondary and tertiary circular reactions in your answer.

5. What is "object permanence"? Describe the *A-not B error* used by Piaget to test the concept of object permanence. According to Piaget's research, at what age do infants acquire this concept?

6. Describe the research that has challenged Piaget's position on object permanence. According to more current research, at what age are infants capable of object permanence? How does Diamond explain the A-not B error observed by Piaget?

7. Describe the research that has investigated recognition memory in infants. At what age are infants able to recognize and remember information and how has this ability been tested?

8. Describe the research that has investigated recall memory in infants. At what age are infants able to recall information and how has this ability been tested? At what age are infants capable of "delayed imitation"?

9. What is "categorization" and what are some of the processes in category formation? Why is categorization an important advancement in cognitive development? At what age are infants able to categorize?

10. Does research indicate that infants see the world as organized into objects? Support your answer with relevant studies.

11. Describe the Bayley Scale of Infant Development. Do scores on the Bayley scale correlate with adult IQ scores? Why or why not?

12. Describe the way in which more recent tests have attempted to measure and predict intelligence. How have measures of habituation and recognition memory been used to measure infant intelligence? What have some of the tests using these measures revealed about the relationship between infant IQ and adult IQ?

MIX-AND-MATCH: In the left-hand column below are some key concepts or definitions. Choose the term from the column on the right that best matches each definition provided in the column on the left.

1. An action that a child performs mentally that is reversible, allowing the person to return mentally to the beginning of the thought sequence

   a. Concrete operations

2. The process that refers to an individual's efforts to deal with the environment by making it fit into the individual's own existing structures

   b. Equilibrium

3. The process whereby concepts are changed in response to environmental demands

   c. Sensorimotor stage

4. The state of cognitive balance that is the result of accommodation

   d. Primary circular reactions

5. The stage of development proposed by Piaget during which cognitive growth is based primarily on sensory experiences and motor actions

   e. Operation

6. The stage of development proposed by Piaget in which the child is first capable of mental representation

   f. Accommodation

7. The stage of development proposed by Piaget in which the child is able to engage in mental operations that are flexible and fully reversible

   g. Object permanence

8. The stage of development proposed by Piaget in which the child is able to reason about hypothetical problems and engage in abstract thinking

   h. Assimilation

9. The understanding or belief that objects continue to exist even when they are out of sight

   i. Category

10. The term used by Piaget to describe a repeated sequence of behavior engaged in by infants that begins initially as a reflex

    j. Tertiary circular reactions

11. The term used by Piaget to describe repeated actions by infants that create interesting sights and sounds, e.g., making a bell ring on a crib

    k. Preoperational stage

12. The term used by Piaget to describe behavioral patterns in which infants vary their actions rather than repeating them while observing their effects on the environment

    l. Formal operations

13. A mental representation of the dimensions that are shared by a set of similar, but not identical, stimuli or events

    m. Secondary circular reactions

MULTIPLE CHOICE QUESTIONS: Read the following questions and indicate your answer by marking the option that you think best answers each question.

1. Which of the following statements regarding Piaget's theory of development is <u>false</u>?
   a. Biology places some limits on the order and speed of cognitive development in children.
   b. Some cognitive ideas, operations, and structures are universal.
   c. Active experience with the world is critical to cognitive growth.
   d. Cognitive development is determined by maturation and is not affected by experience.

2. Piaget's central thesis is that
   a. people are active, curious and inventive throughout life.
   b. cognitive development is solely under the direction of biological factors.
   c. people seek contact with the environment and actively look for a challenge.
   d. both "a" and "c" are true.

3. The process whereby concepts are changed or modified in response to environmental demands is called
   a. adaptation.
   b. accommodation.
   c. assimilation.
   d. equilibration.

4. According to Piaget, the stage of development in which a child is first capable of forming mental representations is the
   a. sensorimotor stage.
   b. preoperational stage.
   c. concrete operational stage.
   d. formal operations stage.

5. Three-month-old Jason repeatedly brushes his fingers against his lips. According to Piaget, Jason's behavior is an example of a
   a. primary circular reaction.
   b. secondary circular reaction.
   c. tertiary circular reaction.
   d. reflex.

6. According to Piaget, infants are not capable of object permanence
   a. until the age of three months.
   b. until the age of six months.
   c. until the age of nine months.
   d. until they no longer make the A-not B error.

7. Current studies suggest that infants are capable of object permanence as early as
   a. one month old.
   b. three months old.
   c. five months old.
   d. nine months old.

8. The type of memory that is first to develop in infants is
   a. recall memory.
   b. recognition memory.
   c. object permanence.
   d. memory for conditioned responses.

9. Current research with infants indicates that memory processes
    a. develop later than Piaget thought.
    b. develop earlier than Piaget thought.
    c. develop at about the age proposed by Piaget.
    d. do not develop until the end of the second year.

10. Research has revealed that infants are capable of "delayed imitation" as young as
    a. one month old.
    b. three months old.
    c. six months old.
    d. nine months old.

TRUE AND FALSE QUESTIONS: Read the following statements and indicate whether you think each statement is true or false.

1. Piaget proposed that infants develop the concept of object permanence by the age of nine months.

2. According to Piaget, infants are first capable of mental representation in the preoperational stage of development.

3. Studies indicate that infants usually develop recall memory by the age of three months.

4. Recent research indicates that infants too young to grasp are able to see the world as organized into objects.

5. The Bayley Scale of Infant Development accurately predicts intelligence in adulthood.

6. Individual assessments of habituation and recognition memory reliably predict IQ scores in childhood.

7. According to Piaget, tertiary circular reactions first emerge in the concrete operational stage of development.

8. Piaget believed that some cognitive ideas, operations and structures are universal.

9. The ability to recognize and place objects into categories does not emerge until the age of two years.

10. Research in developmental psychology has not disputed any of Piaget's original research or theoretical positions.

FILL-IN-THE-BLANKS: Read the following sentences and write the missing word or words in the space provided.

1. Developmental psychologists make a distinction between children's _____, or the knowledge and skills that they possess, and their _____, or the actual demonstration of knowledge and skills in observable problem-solving situations.

2. Piaget believed that both _____ and _____ were critical to cognitive growth.

3. According to Piaget, _____ and _____ are the two basic principles guiding human development.

4. The process of adaptation occurs through two complementary processes which Piaget referred to as _____ and _____.

5. According to Piaget, cognitive growth in the sensorimotor stage is based primarily on _____ and _____.

6. Piaget referred to the repeated sequences of behavior in infants that develop originally from reflexes as _____; repeated actions that create interesting sights and sounds as _____; and the systematic variation of actions that explore the effect on the infant's environment as _____.

7. According to Piaget, infants do not have a concept of _____ i.e., the ability to recognize that objects still exist when no longer in sight, until they no longer make the _____.

8. Tests that measure _____ and _____ in infants have been shown to predict IQ scores reliably in _____.

9. A _____ is defined as a mental representation of the dimensions that are shared by a set of similar, but not identical, stimuli or events.

10. Currents research suggests that young children and infants are more likely to categorize objects in the world _____ than according to _____ relations.

MIX-AND-MATCH

1.	e	2.	h
3.	f	4.	b
5.	c	6.	k
7.	a	8.	l
9.	g	10.	d
11.	m	12.	j
13.	i		

MULTIPLE CHOICE

1.	d	2.	d
3.	b	4.	b
5.	a	6.	d
7.	c	8.	b
9.	b	10.	d

TRUE AND FALSE

1.	false	2.	true
3.	false	4.	true
5.	false	6.	true
7.	false	8.	true
9.	false	10.	false

FILL-IN-THE-BLANKS

1. competence; performance
2. maturation; experience
3. organization; adaptation
4. assimilation; accommodation
5. sensory experience; motor actions
6. primary circular reactions; secondary circular reactions; tertiary circular reactions
7. object permanence; A-not B error
8. habituation; recognition memory; childhood
9. category
10. taxonomically; thematic

CHAPTER 6

EMOTIONAL AND SOCIAL DEVELOPMENT IN INFANCY

CHAPTER OVERVIEW

To study emotional development in infants, researchers study facial expressions and changes in the body and brain that are normally associated with emotions in adults. Research has revealed facial expressions corresponding to sadness and surprise in infants as young as four months old. Although smiling is sometimes a reflex, infants may smile in response to specific stimuli, such as human faces, within the first two months, and by the age of 10 months, "felt" smiles produce brain activity that is typically associated with positive emotions. Infants develop specific fears from about 7 to 12 months of age. For example, fear of unexpected events and strangers emerges during this period. Separation fear occurs when infants are temporarily separated from their primary caregiver, causing anxiety and distress, and appears to universal. Fear of sudden drops of height emerges at around eight months and appears to be related to changes in locomotion skills rather than to changes in depth perception.

Researchers also have been interested in determining whether specific personality traits remain stable over time. Studies reveal that in general, activity level and irritability in infancy do not persist over time. The tendency either to be inhibited or uninhibited appears to be relatively stable over time, however. Longitudinal studies reveal that individuals who are inhibited as children tend to be shy and reserved as adults and individuals who are uninhibited as children tend to be more outgoing and sociable as adults. However, most developmental psychologists acknowledge that, in addition to inherent traits, personality also is influenced by the traits and characteristics of the primary caregivers and other socializing agents.

Theories differ in their explanations of emotional and social development. Freud believed that too much or too little stimulation in a given stage of development may cause an individual to become "fixated" and may impede the individual's psychological and social development. Erikson emphasized the importance of social interactions in personality development, e.g., the development of trust in the first year. Learning theorists argue that behavior and "personality" are not due to inborn traits but are the product of learned associations that are acquired over time. Research in ethology has revealed that some species are born with "fixed action patterns" that are triggered by specific stimuli, which has contributed to the development of attachment theory.

According to attachment theory, infants are born with specific behaviors that elicit nurturing responses from their caregiver and promote attachment. Researchers have identified four attachment styles. Children who are easily comforted by their caregiver when distressed are classified as securely attached. Children who reject and avoid their caregivers are classified as avoidant. Children who alternate between avoidant and clinging behavior are classified as resistant. Finally, children who do not seem to fit any of the categories are classified as disorganized. Although attachment styles often predict specific behavioral outcomes, these classifications should not be considered immutable. Research has revealed that attachment styles can be modified by changes in the child's social environment. Theorists also acknowledge that personality and behavior may be due more to a child's temperament than to his or her attachment.

The traits of caregivers play an important role in the development of attachment styles. Studies indicate that securely attached children tend to have parents who respond to them in a sensitive and timely manner. Insecure children often have caregivers who are insensitive to their needs or inconsistent in their response to them. Studies do not support the view that nonmaternal attachments necessarily interfere with children's primary attachment to their mother, although the quality of nonmaternal care can play an important role in children's social development. Finally, researchers continue to study the role that culture plays in a child's social development.

CHAPTER OUTLINE: Use the outline provided below by writing information related to each topic in the margins of the outline, e.g., definitions of terms and elaboration of concepts.

I. Emotion in Infancy

A. *The meaning of emotion*

B. *Inferring emotions in infancy*

C. *Fears of infancy*

II. Temperamental Differences in Infants

A. *Activity level*

B. *Irritability*

C. *Reaction to unfamiliarity*

D. *The principle of bidirectionality*

III. Emotional and Social Relationships with Adults

A. *Psychoanalytic theory*

B. *Learning theory*

C. *Ethology*

D. *Attachment theory*

E. *Measuring attachment*

F. *Caregiving and attachment*

IV. Consequences of Variations in Caregiving Arrangements

A. *Institutional care*

B. *Partial nonmaternal care*

V. Cultural Ideals and Child Rearing

A. *Cultural differences in conception of ideal child*

B. *Japanese vs. American differences in parenting styles*

KEY DEFINITIONS AND TERMS: Define the following concepts and terms Try to provide an example for each word or term you have defined to help clarify its meaning.

Emotion:

Felt smile:

Unfelt smile:

Stranger anxiety:

Separation anxiety:

Visual cliff:

Social referencing:

Temperament:

Inhibited vs. uninhibited traits:

Bidirectionality:

Libido:

Anal stage:

Autonomous:

Ethology:

Fixed-action patterns:

Attachment:

Strange situation:

Secure attachment:

Insecure attachment:

Avoidant attachment:

Resistant attachment:

Disorganized attachment:

Adult Attachment Interview:

Autonomous patterns of recall:

Dismissing patterns of recall:

Preoccupied patterns of recall:

Partial nonmaternal care:

REVIEW QUESTIONS: Below are questions that relate to key concepts and information covered in your textbook. Answer the questions as thoroughly and completely as possible. Try to provide examples to support your answer and to clarify meaning.

1. Describe some of the procedures that researchers have used to infer emotions in infancy. At what age do facial expressions of surprise, sadness, fear and anger first emerge? How might emotional responses to the same stimuli change over time?

2. Describe the research that has studied smiling in infants. What are the various stimuli that tend to evoke smiling in infants and at what age? What type of smile is associated with self-reports of happiness?

3. Discuss the way in which environmental contingencies and reinforcements influence the frequency of smiling. Cite relevant research to support your answer.

4. At what age do fears in infancy first emerge and what type of event is most likely to cause fear in infants? At what age does fear of strangers first emerge and under what conditions are strangers most likely to evoke a fearful response in infants?

5. Describe the research that has investigated separation fear during infancy. At what age does separation anxiety first emerge, when does it peak, and under what conditions is it most likely to occur? Does separation anxiety appear to be universal or is it culture-specific?

6. Describe research that has used the "visual cliff" to test fear of sudden drops in height. When do infants first develop this fear and why? Discuss the way in which infants rely on "social referencing" when deciding whether to cross the deep side of the visual cliff.

7. Why are psychologists interested in studying temperament and what two criteria have been used to assess which temperamental dimensions are important? Describe the research on temperament conducted by Alexander Thomas and Stella Chess. What were the three temperaments that they identified in babies? What type of babies were most likely to develop serious emotional problems as children?

8. Describe the research that has investigated the following characteristics of infants' temperaments: activity level, irritability and reaction to unfamiliarity. Which of the temperaments tend to persist over time? Cite relevant studies to support your answer.

9. Discuss the principle of bidirectionality in development. How can the temperament of both the parents and child affect social and emotional development? Provide an example to support your answer.

10. Discuss Freud's theoretical perspective and his explanation regarding emotional and social development during infancy. How did Erikson differ from Freud in his view of social and emotional development in children?

11. Discuss learning theory's explanation of emotional and social development. According to this view, how and why do infants develop emotional ties to their mother? Did the research with rhesus monkeys conducted by Harry Harlow confirm or refute the behavioral view that love and attachment are primarily the result of conditioning?

12. Describe the major tenets of ethology and the research that has been conducted in this field. How did ethology contribute to the development of attachment theory?

13. Discuss the major tenets of attachment theory. What three phenomena are signs of an infant's attachment? Under what conditions are infants likely to display attachment behaviors?

14. Describe the procedure developed by Mary Ainsworth used to assess attachment, the three patterns of attachment reported by Ainsworth, and the fourth pattern that recently has been added. Discuss the way in which attachment patterns predict behavior at a later age.

15. Discuss the limitations of the "strange situation" in assessing attachment styles. Are attachment styles immutable or can they be modified? In what way might temperament and culture affect a child's behavior in the strange situation? How might the degree to which parents encourage their children to control fear in the first year influence a child's behavior in the strange situation?

16. Discuss the traits and characteristics of parents who have securely attached children. What three qualities of social interactions between parent and child are most important for the development of attachment?

17. Discuss the role of the father in the attachment process. Do fathers have the capacity to provide appropriate and sensitive care to infants? What types of interactions do fathers typically have with their infants?

18. According to Belsky and Isabella (1988), what three classes of variables are related to attachment security? What evidence have Belsky and Isabella provided to support their position?

19. Describe the Adult Attachment Interview developed by Mary Main and her colleagues and the three patterns of perceived attachment that they identified. How do the characteristics of parents measured by the AAI correspond to the attachment styles of their infants?

20. Discuss some of the possible outcomes in the social and emotional development of children raised in institutions. Are the long-term consequences of being institutionalized always negative?

21. Discuss the two controversial issues surrounding partial nonmaternal care. Does research support or refute the "one mother" hypothesis? Discuss the way in which the quality of nonmaternal care can affect the social and emotional development of children.

22. Discuss the way in which cultural ideals of children affect parenting. How have attitudes toward child rearing changed in American culture in the past 70 years?

MIX-AND-MATCH: In the left-hand column below are some key concepts or definitions. Choose the term from the column on the right that best matches each definition provided in the column on the left.

1. A conscious awareness of a specific change in internal feeling tone

    a. Resistant

2. An individual's inborn bias toward certain moods and reaction styles

    b. Avoidant attachment

3. The idea that parent-child relationships interact and affect a child's social and emotional development

    c. Learning theory

4. Type of attachment in which children actively seek parents and are easily comforted by the parent when they are distressed

    d. Disorganized

5. Type of attachment in which children show little interest if the parent leaves and ignore the parent when he or she returns

    e. Psychoanalytic theory

6. Type of attachment in which children alternately cling and avoid their parent after the parent returns following a brief separation

    f. Emotion

7. Type of attachment in which children in the strange situation do not seem to fit any of the available categories

    g. Autonomous

8. Secure pattern of remembering childhood attachments, which is also referred to as "free to recall"

    h. Temperament

9. Pattern of remembering childhood attachments in which individuals deny the importance of their attachments

    i. Ethology

10. Pattern of remembering childhood attachment in which children often idealize their parents but without being able to remember concrete evidence

    j. Principle of bidirectionality

11. Theory which proposes that fixation in a particular stage can impede an individual's social and emotional development

    k. Preoccupied

12. Theory that focuses on biological drives and on measureable behavior in its explanation of social and emotional development

    l. Dismissing

13. Field that studies inborn tendencies, such as fixed action patterns in various species, and has contributed to the development of attachment theory

    m. Secure attachment

Read the following questions and indicate your answer by marking the option that you think best answers each question.

1. A study that investigated the frequency of smiling in infants raised in three different environments in Israel found that
    a. institutionalized infants did not begin smiling until after the age of 12 months.
    b. kibbutz infants smiled less frequently than institutionalized infants after the first year.
    c. institutionalized infants smiled less frequently than kibbutz infants after the first year.
    d. kibbutz infants did not begin smiling until after six months.

2. Fear that infants experience on the "visual cliff"
    a. does not emerge until approximately the age of two years.
    b. is caused by changes in the infant's depth perception.
    c. does not emerge until the infant begins to creep or crawl.
    d. both "a" and "b" are true.

3. The type of temperament that appears to remain stable over time is
    a. activity level.
    b. fear of strangers.
    c. inhibition vs. disinhibition.
    d. irritability.

4. Attachment research on rhesus monkeys conducted by Harry Harlow revealed that
    a. infant monkeys preferred the wire mother and usually rejected the terry cloth mother.
    b. infants monkeys often developed an extreme fear of the terry cloth mother.
    c. infant monkeys preferred the terry cloth mother over the wire mother when frightened.
    d. both "a" and "b" are true are true.

5. Children who ignore their parent following his or her return in the "strange situation" are
    a. securely attached.
    b. avoidant.
    c. resistant.
    d. disorganized.

6. Which of the following is not a limitation of the strange situation cited in your book?
    a. Classifications are not immutable and often change.
    b. Temperament and the cultural values may affect attachment classifications.
    c. The nervous system may cause a child to be unusually reactive to changes in stimulation.
    d. The "strange situation" test cannot adequately assess attachment styles.

7. According to Mary Main and her colleagues, individuals who often idealize their parents but without being able to remember concrete supporting evidence can be classified as
    a. autonomous.
    b. preoccupied.
    c. dismissing.
    d. disorganized.

8. According to Belsky and Isabella, which of the following variables are not related to attachment security?
    a. the mother's personality before giving birth
    b. the parent's socio-economic status
    c. the infant's temperament
    d. characteristics of the marriage

9. Research that has investigating the effect of nonmaternal care on infant attachment has revealed that
   a. nonmaternal care such as "day care" significantly interferes with the attachment process.
   b. nonmaternal care interferes with cognitive and socioemotional development.
   c. nonmaternal care does not interfere with infant-parent attachments.
   d. day care facilities in the United States all maintain high standards in quality of care.

10. Cross-cultural and historical research on child rearing practices have revealed that
   a. the majority of cultures are extremely similar in their cultural ideals and child rearing.
   b. attitudes regarding child rearing in the U. S. have changed very little in the last 70 years.
   c. Japanese tend to focus on building a close loyalty to and dependence on the mother.
   d. Japanese mothers are more likely to foster independence than American mothers.

TRUE AND FALSE QUESTIONS: Read the following statements and indicate whether you think each statement is true or false.

1. Felt smiles do not occur in infants prior to the age of one.

2. Avoidance of the apparently deep side of the "visual cliff" is due to a new ability in the infant to perceive depth.

3. Research indicates that separation fear appears to be a universal phenomenon.

4. Studies on temperament indicate that irritability in the first six months of infancy is a reliable predictor of irritability in childhood and adulthood.

5. Studies indicate that partial nonmaternal care interferes significantly with infant-parent attachments.

6. Observations of fathers in standardized situations reveal that they show as much sensitivity, affection and skill as their wives when feeding and holding their newborn infants.

7. Studies indicate that "preoccupied" parents tend to have resistant babies.

8. Individuals who are inhibited as infants tend to be socially outgoing as children and adults.

9. Most psychologists agree that children's inborn temperaments will determine their personality regardless of their upbringing or interaction with their parents.

10. Fixed-action patterns are learned responses that are acquired through experience.

FILL-IN-THE-BLANKS: Read the following sentences and write the missing word or words in the space provided.

1. To study emotions in infants, researchers in developmental psychology have focused on changes in _____ and _____.

2. The two criteria that have been used to assess which temperamental dimensions are most important are whether they are _____ and whether they are based on _____ or _____ factors.

3. Longitudinal studies indicate that individuals who are _____ at a young age tend to be shy and timid at later ages, and individuals who are _____ at a young age tend to be socially outgoing at later ages.

4. According to ethologists, animals are born with a set of _____ that are set in motion when the proper environmental stimulus, called a _____, occurs.

5. According to Ainsworth, infants in the "strange situation" who ignore their mother following her return are _____, infants who alternately cling and avoid their mother are _____, and infants who are easily comforted by their mother when distressed are _____.

6. The three elements of social interaction that are most important for the development of attachment are _____, _____ and _____.

7. According to Main's classifications on the AAI, adults who are "free to recall" their childhood attachments are _____, those who deny the importance of attachment are _____, and those who idealize their parents but who are unable to provide concrete evidence are _____.

8. The _____ is the belief that attachment to the primary caregiver may be disrupted if infants spend many hours a day in the care of someone other than the _____.

9. The _____ is an apparatus that is used to assess early depth perception and has been used to study an infant's fear of sudden changes in _____.

10. The term temperament refers to the inborn biases toward certain _____ and _____.

MIX-AND-MATCH

1.	f	2.	h
3.	j	4.	m
5.	b	6.	a
7.	d	8.	g
9.	l	10.	k
11.	e	12.	c
13.	i		

MULTIPLE CHOICE

1.	c	2.	c
3.	c	4.	c
5.	b	6.	d
7.	b	8.	b
9.	c	10.	c

TRUE AND FALSE

1.	false	2.	false
3.	true	4.	false
5.	false	6.	true
7.	true	8.	false
9.	false	10.	false

FILL-IN-THE-BLANKS

1. brain activity; facial expressions
2. stable over time; inherited; prenatal physiological
3. inhibited; uninhibited
4. fixed-action patterns; releaser
5. avoidant; resistant; secure
6. sensitivity; synchrony; reciprocity
7. autonomous; dismissing; preoccupied
8. one mother hypothesis; biological mother
9. visual cliff; height
10. moods; reaction styles

CHAPTER 7:
THE SECOND AND THIRD YEARS

CHAPTER OVERVIEW

Children go through significant changes in the second and third year of their life. One notable change is their ability to engage in symbolic play. Beginning in the second year, children are able to use their imagination to symbolically transform ordinary objects into "play" objects. They also begin to include toys as symbolic agents in their play, e.g., having two dolls interact and play roles. Symbolic play stimulates the development of more complex cognitive and motor skills and also facilitates social interactions. After the first year, children begin to make the transition from solitary play to interactive pretend play with other children, although play activity that includes elaborate role-playing scenarios and established rules does not begin until the age of three or four.

Another skill that develops between ages one and three is the ability to imitate an observed action of another person. Although imitation may begin as early as 11 months, it becomes more frequent and complex after the first year. Imitation facilitates cognitive and technical development and plays an important role in human adaptation and survival. It is rare in other species other than humans and appears to be universal. Four hypotheses related to imitation have been offered. First, social and parental approval promotes imitation in infants. Second, imitation enhances similarities children have with other people. Third, children are most likely to imitate individuals who are important sources of emotional arousal, e.g., parents. Finally, observing and imitating goal-directed behavior of others allows children to achieve similar goals.

Children's artistic abilities and expression also become more symbolic during the second and third year. Artistic abilities of children from different cultures appear to develop in a particular sequence, beginning with crude scribbles at 16 months to dots or lines representing eyes and nose surrounded by a circle by the age of 30 months. One important ability that develops after the second year is the ability to conceptualize models as representations of real objects. Studies have shown that the ability to recognize a scaled down or miniature version of an object does not emerge until after the age of two-and-a-half when representation skills first begin to develop.

Research on self-awareness has revealed that most children are able to recognize themselves in a mirror by the age of 24 months. Moreover, the use of pronouns, such as I, me, and you, also begins around this time, indicating that children have developed the ability to distinguish themselves from other people. Because deaf children begin to use signs to refer to themselves at approximately the same age as hearing children, researchers have come to the conclusion that self-awareness may be under the direction of maturation. Studies also reveal that a sense of possession begins to develop at about the same time self-awareness first emerges.

As early as the second year, children begin to develop empathy, i.e., the ability to understand and appreciate the feelings and perceptions of others. During the second six months of the second year, children also begin to develop idealized standards of various objects and events and may show signs of concern if they encounter something that violates a particular standard. They often experiment with rule violations during this period and may joke about bodily functions and sex-appropriate behavior. Although parents may find this developmental period particularly challenging, both compliance and the ability to tolerate delays improve during this period as children mature and become more cognitively advanced. Developmental theorists have proposed that dimensions of warmth and control vary and combine to produce four parenting styles. Authoritarian parents are demanding but low on warmth, authoritative parents are controlling but high in warmth. Permissive parents are high on warmth and undemanding, and rejecting-neglecting parents are low on both dimensions. Research indicates that establishing a warm and affectionate relationship and exerting firm control have the most positive developmental outcome.

CHAPTER OUTLINE: Use the outline provided below by writing information related to each topic in the margins of the outline, e.g., definitions of terms and elaboration of concepts.

I. **Symbolic Ability**

    A. *Symbolic play*

    B. *The role of symbolic play*

    C. *Imitation*

    D. *Hypotheses about the determinants of imitation*

    E. *Drawing*

    F. *Seeing models as representations*

II. **The Onset of Self-Awareness**

    A. *Self-recognition*

    B. *Describing one's own behavior*

    C. *A sense of possession*

III. **Empathy and a Moral Sense**

    A. *Empathy*

    B. *Standards*

    C. *Violations of rules*

IV. **Family Interactions in the Second and Third Years**

    A. *Toilet training*

    B. *Parenting styles*

    C. *Authoritative parents*

    D. *Authoritarian parents*

    E. *Permissive parents*

    F. *Rejecting-neglecting parents*

KEY DEFINITIONS AND TERMS: Define the following concepts and terms Try to provide an example for each word or term you have defined to help clarify its meaning.

Symbolic ability:

Play:

Imitation:

Models as representations:

Self-awareness:

Sense of Possession:

Empathy:

Standards:

Authoritative parents:

Authoritarian parents:

Permissive parents:

Rejecting-neglecting parents:

REVIEW QUESTIONS: Below are questions that relate to key concepts and information covered in your textbook. Answer the questions as thoroughly and completely as possible. Try to provide examples to support your answer and to clarify meaning.

1. What are the four criteria that most observers use in defining play? Describe the way in which play activities of children change in the second and third year of life.

2. What are some of the important functions that play activities have? Discuss the role that play activity has in children's emotional, cognitive, and social development.

3. Discuss the role that imitation plays in children's cognitive and social development. Whom are children most likely to imitate? Do imitation abilities appear to be due to maturation or learning? Is the emergence of this ability universal or culture-specific? Are autistic children as capable of imitation as children who are not autistic?

4. Describe the four hypotheses about the determinants of imitation that are cited in your textbook.

5. Describe the way in which children's drawing changes in the second and third year. When does a child's ability to conceptualize models as representations first develop?

6. Describe the research that has investigated self-recognition in children. At what age does self-awareness in most children first emerge? Does self-awareness develop at the same approximate age in deaf children as it does in hearing children?

7. Describe the way in which children's self-descriptions change as they grow older. Discuss some of the explanations as to why children are more likely to describe their own activities than the behaviors of others?

8. Why and when do children develop a sense of possession? Discuss the way in which culture and the values of the society in which the child is raised can modify a child's possessiveness.

9. What is empathy and when do signs of empathy first emerge in children? Does empathy appear to develop earlier or later than Piaget proposed?

10. What are "standards" and at what age do children begin to develop them? What are the typical reactions children have if an object or event violates a particular standard? What are the typical reactions children have if they are unable to meet standards of behavior imposed by others?

11. At what age do children become more interested in exploring violations of adult rules? Provide examples of some of the ways two-year-olds might "test the limits" of rule violations.

12. Discuss some of the challenges parents have in raising children in the second to third year. In a study conducted by Minton, Kagan, and Levine (1971), how frequently did "violation sequences" occur between mother and child per hour? Do children become better or worse in their capacity to "obey and delay"?

13. Discuss some of the ways in which a child's own temperament and personality can affect parent-child interactions and discipline. How can parental, social, and cultural values also affect parental expectations and child-rearing practices?

14. Describe the two dimensions that define parenting styles and the way in which Baumrind proposes they combine to produce the following: authoritative parents, authoritarian parents, permissive parents, and rejecting-neglecting parents.

MIX-AND-MATCH: In the left-hand column below are some key concepts or definitions. Choose the term from the column on the right that best matches each definition provided in the column on the left.

1. The ability to create and accept arbitrary relationships between objects and ideas and let one thing stand for another

   a. Standards

2. Observing and repeating the actions and behaviors of another person

   b. Authoritative parents

3. The capacity individuals have to perceive their own qualities, states, and abilities

   c. Permissive parents

4. The ability to appreciate the perceptions and feelings of others

   d. Warmth

5. Idealized representations that individuals have of objects, events, and behaviors

   e. Authoritarian parents

6. A dimension on which parents can vary from accepting, responsive, and child-centered to rejecting, unresponsive, and parent-centered

   f. Symbolic ability

7. Type of parents who are undemanding and who are also low in warmth

   g. Rejecting-neglecting parents

8. Type of parents who are demanding and who are low in warmth

   h. Imitation

9. Type of parents who are high in firm control but who are high in warmth

   i. Self-awareness

10. Type of parents who are high in warmth but who are undemanding

   j. Empathy

MULTIPLE CHOICE QUESTIONS: Read the following questions and indicate your answer by marking the option that you think best answers each question.

1. Which of the following is <u>not</u> a criterion that most observers use in defining play?
   a. Play is pleasurable and enjoyable.
   b. Play has extrinsic goals in which the child's motivations serve a practical purpose.
   c. Play is spontaneous and voluntary, freely chosen by the player.
   d. Play involves some active engagement on the part of the player.

2. Changes in symbolic play and sequences of development in symbolic play
   a. occur at about the same time in children regardless of culture.
   b. have also been observed in deaf children, whose play is less directed by language.
   c. differ significantly depending on the child's cultural and social environment.
   d. incorporate both "a" and "b."

3. Which of the following is <u>not</u> a hypothesized determinant of imitation cited in your book?
   a. Social and parental reinforcement promote imitation in infants.
   b. Imitation is a way of establishing and enhancing similarity to another person.
   c. Children imitate their parents because parents are a constant source of emotional arousal.
   d. Children are more likely to imitate strangers than parents.

4. A two-year-old child who is able to find a hidden toy in an ordinary-size room, but who is unable to find a miniature version of the toy in a scaled-down version of the room, is incapable of
   a. engaging in symbolic play.
   b. seeing models as representations.
   c. sorting items into categories.
   d. delayed imitation.

5. The majority of children are able to recognize themselves in the mirror by
   a. six months.
   b. the end of the first year.
   c. 24 months.
   d. the age of three years.

6. Research on self-descriptive behavior has revealed that two-year-olds
   a. are more likely to describe their own activities than the behaviors of others.
   b. are more likely to describe the activities of others than their own behavior.
   c. are incapable of self-referencing because they have not developed self-awareness.
   d. exhibit both "b" and "c."

7. Signs of empathy in children emerge
   a. much later than Piaget originally proposed.
   b. no earlier than the age of three years.
   c. sometime toward the second birthday.
   d. as stated om both "a" and "b."

8. A study by Minton, Kagan, and Levine found that "violation sequences" between mothers and their 27-month-olds occurred approximately
   a. once an hour.
   b. three times an hour.
   c. nine times an hour.
   d. six times per day.

9. According to Baumrind, parents who are high in warmth but who are undemanding are
   a. authoritarian.
   b. authoritative.
   c. permissive.
   d. rejecting-neglecting.

10. According to Baumrind, parents who are low in warmth but who are demanding of their children are
    a. authoritarian.
    b. authoritative.
    c. permissive.
    d. rejecting-neglecting.

TRUE AND FALSE QUESTIONS: Read the following statements and indicate whether you think each statement is true or false.

1. The sequences of development in symbolic play of deaf children are similar to the sequences in hearing children.

2. Research has revealed that changes in symbolic play with objects across age occur at about the same time across very different cultures.

3. Imitation is not unique to humans and is quite common in other species.

4. Children more often imitate their parents than other adults.

5. The majority of children are able to recognize themselves in a mirror by the end of the first year.

6. Research has revealed that children do not show signs of empathy until the end of the third year.

7. Children are unable to see models as representations until the age of two-and-a-half to three years of age.

8. Children who attain a sense of self-awareness a little earlier than other children are usually more possessive.

9. The age at which an appreciation of "right" and "wrong" behaviors appears is remarkably similar in children from many different cultures and families.

10. According to Baumrind, parents who are demanding but low in warmth are authoritative.

FILL-IN-THE-BLANKS: Read the following sentences and write the missing word or words in the space provided.

1. The _____ of humans includes many different capacities to create and accept arbitrary relationships between objects and ideas.

2. Changes in symbolic play with objects across age occur at about the same time across very different _____. Similar sequences of development have been observed in _____ children, whose play may be less directed by language.

3. The four proposed hypotheses about the determinants of imitation are that imitation promotes social _____, enhances _____ to another, that _____ is a basis for imitating and imitation allows individuals to gain _____.

4. A capacity that develops from ages one to three that has been linked to symbolic ability is children's selective _____, or ability to duplicate particular observed actions of others.

5. During the last half of the second year, children begin to have _____, a capacity to perceive their own qualities, states, and abilities.

6. The emergence of self-awareness is accompanied by the occurrence of _____, the ability to appreciate the perceptions and feelings of others.

7. During the last six months of the second year, children begin to create _____, idealized representations of objects, events, and behaviors.

8. As children grow from infancy into childhood, they become more likely to be interested in exploring violations of adult _____ that will provoke disgust or disapproval in others.

9. The dimension on which parents can vary from accepting and responsive to rejecting and unresponsive can be labeled _____.

10. Parents who are high in warmth and firm in control are _____, parents who are low in warmth and high in control are _____, parents who are undemanding but high in warmth are _____, and parents who are low on both dimensions are _____.

MIX-AND-MATCH

1. f	2. h
3. i	4. j
5. a	6. d
7. g	8. e
9. b	10. c

MULTIPLE CHOICE

1. b	2. d
3. d	4. b
5. c	6. a
7. c	8. c
9. c	10. a

TRUE AND FALSE

1. true	2. true
3. false	4. true
5. false	6. false
7. true	8. true
9. true	10. false

FILL-IN-THE-BLANKS

1. symbolic abilities
2. cultures; deaf
3. interactions; similarities; emotional arousal; goals
4. imitation
5. self-awareness
6. empathy
7. standards
8. rules
9. warmth
10. authoritative; authoritarian; permissive; rejecting-neglecting

CHAPTER 8:
LANGUAGE AND COMMUNICATION

CHAPTER OVERVIEW

The English language has 40 phonemes, the basic sound units that combine to make words. Habituation studies reveal that infants are born with the ability to discriminate between similar phonemes, giving them the capacity to learn a variety of languages. Despite this ability, infants do not begin to "babble" until five or six months of age. Babbling increases in frequency until the end of the first year, when infants speak their first words.

Research indicates that children usually understand more words than they speak. The meaning that they give to words may not always be accurate, however. Children often overgeneralize the meaning of a word, e.g., refer to all four-legged animals as a dog, which are called "overextensions." Conversely, "underextensions" are errors in meaning that occur if the child's definition of a word is too narrow or restrictive. Overextensions do not usually reflect errors in children's comprehension of word meanings, however, only errors in their production of words.

Psychologists have been interested in determining how children assign meaning to words. One way children learn is by listening to adults name various objects. In general, children learn words at the "basic" level first and learn specific words later. Children also have the tendency to label unfamiliar objects with unfamiliar names, sometimes referred to as the "novel name-nameless category" principle. Another principle of learning is the "whole-object assumption," which is the tendency for children to assume that a word refers to an entire object and not its parts. Finally, the taxonomic assumption is a principle that refers to the tendency for children to assume that word labels that apply to a particular object will also apply to similar objects.

Children begin to express simple relations between words and concepts at around the middle of the second year. Sentences tend to be simple, containing only those words that are essential to its meaning. The smallest grammatical units of meaning are called morphemes, which can either stand alone or as parts of words. Children learn grammatical morphemes in a particular order, which becomes gradually more complex. Many theorists believe that children learn grammatical rules rather than simply memorize a long list of words. For example, children may add -ed to a word to indicate past tense (e.g., "I goed) a phenomenon referred to as over-regularization.

From ages two to four, children begin to develop more complex syntax, such as constructing and combining complex sentences, formulating questions, using deictic words, using passive sentences, and using negative sentences correctly. An important advancement is the ability to use language in its proper physical social context, an aspect of language called pragmatics. Piaget believed that children were incapable of "socialized" speech until the age of six or seven but current research reveals that basic socialized speech may begin as early as the age of two.

Several theories of language acquisition have been proposed. Learning theory contends that language is under the direction of basic learning principles, although psycholinguists argue that these principles do not fully explain language acquisition. Nativist theory stresses that language acquisition is under the control of biological influences, arguing that many aspects of language development are universal and that evidence of "critical periods" indicates an innate biological readiness for language. Some nativists believe that humans have innate brain mechanisms that specialize in language acquisition, whereas other nativists maintain that humans are born with basic cognitive functions and motivational predispositions that facilitate but are not specific to language development. The validity of each view continues to be debated as researchers and theorists focus on relevant issues, e.g, the extent to which children get negative feedback from their parents and the extent to which language is child-directed. Neither view has been refuted.

CHAPTER OUTLINE: Use the outline provided below by writing information related to each topic in the margins of the outline, e.g., definitions of terms and elaboration of concepts.

I. **A Description of Language Acquisition**

   A. *Phonemes and babbling*

   B. *Perceiving phonemes and linguistic structure*

   C. *Babbling*

II. **Semantics: Learning the Meanings of Words**

   A. *First words*

   B. *The process of word learning*

III. **Syntax: Combining Words into Sentences**

   A. *First word combinations*

   B. *Learning syntactic rules*

   C. *Development of complex syntax*

IV. **Pragmatics: Language in Context**

   A. *The development of socialized speech*

   B. *Piaget vs. current theory*

V. **Explanations of Language Acquisition**

   A. *Learning theory*

   B. *Nativist theory*

   C. *Critical periods*

   D. *Two kinds of nativist theory*

   E. *Theoretical controversies*

KEY DEFINITIONS AND TERMS: Define the following concepts and terms Try to provide an example for each word or term you have defined to help clarify its meaning.

Phonemes:

Babbling:

Word comprehension:

Semantics:

Overextensions:

Underextensions:

Novel name-nameless category principle:

Whole-object assumption:

Taxonomic assumption:

Syntax:

Morphemes:

Unbound morphemes:

Bound morphemes:

Over-regularization:

Mean length of utterance:

Deictic words:

Passive sentences:

Negatives:

Pragmatics:

Learning theory:

Nativist theory:

Critical periods:

Inside-out nativist theory:

Outside-in nativist theory:

Language acquisition device:

Negative Feedback:

Child-directed language:

Below are questions that relate to key concepts and information covered in your textbook. Answer the questions as thoroughly and completely as possible. Try to provide examples to support your answer and to clarify meaning.

1. What are the functions of language? Discuss some of the ways in which humans use language to communicate, establish and maintain relationships with others, demarcate categories, and aid in inference and deduction.

2. What are phonemes and how many are there in the English language? How has research investigated an infant's ability to discriminate between similar phoneme, and at what age does this ability first occur? How do language and culture affect an infant's ability to discriminate phonemes?

3. When do infants first produce vowel sounds, when does babbling begin, and when does babbling begin to decrease in frequency? Does babbling appear to be due to maturational or environmental influences?

4. Does the frequency of babbling predict how early or late normal children will speak words or the size of their vocabulary when they enter school? Discuss the research that supports the position that babbling reflects a child's degree of excitability and tendency to express excitement in vocal sounds.

5. When do infants speak their first meaningful sounds and what types of words are most likely to be spoken first? What other types of words do children seem to prefer when they first begin to talk? Do children learn words at the same pace or is there variation in the rate at which children learn words? How do parents and a child's gender affect variations in speed of vocabulary development?

6. What is the difference between word production and word comprehension? Do children produce more words than they understand or do they understand more words than they produce?

7. Describe some of the errors children make when attributing meaning to words. What are overextensions and underextensions? Do these errors reflect children's comprehension of a word? Why do these errors occur?

8. Discuss the following ways in which children learn words: Naming rituals, the N3C principle, the whole-object assumption principle, and the taxonomic assumption principle.

9. Discuss the order in which children learn syntactic rules. What evidence is there that children learn rules that aid them in language acquisition rather than simply memorize long lists of words?

10. Describe how psychologists compute the average length of a sample of utterances by use of the MLU. What technique is currently used to estimate syntactic competence ?

11. Describe the way in which children learn the following grammatical complexities in the years from two to four: Combining sentences, producing and comprehending questions, using and understanding deictic words, using the passive voice, and using negatives correctly.

12. To what does the term "pragmatics" refer? According to Piaget, do young children possess the cognitive capacities needed to develop communication skills at this level? At what age did Piaget believe children are first capable of "socialized" speech? Does current research support or refute Piaget's position?

13. According to learning theory, how do children acquire language? What are the criticisms that developmental psycholinguists have of learning theory's view of language acquisition?

14. Describe the nativist theory of language acquisition and research evidence that supports this position. What is meant by a "critical period" of language development? Did Genie's progress in language development tend to support or refute the critical period view?

15. What are the two kinds of nativist theory and how do they differ in their assumptions about language development?

16. Discuss the following two issues on which nativists disagree: Negative feedback and child-directed language. Why are negative feedback and child-directed language theoretically important issues?

MIX-AND-MATCH: In the left-hand column below are some key concepts or definitions. Choose the term from the column on the right that best matches each definition provided in the column on the left.

1. The basic sound units that are combined to make words

   a. N3C principle

2. The meaning system of a language

   b. Overextensions

3. Errors in language in which applications of meanings are too wide

   c. Pragmatics

4. Errors in language in which word meaning is defined too narrowly

   d. Outside-in theory

5. The principle that refers to a child's tendency to label an unfamiliar object with an unfamiliar name

   e. Syntax

6. The tendency for children to first assume that a word refers to a whole object and not its parts

   f. Morphemes

7. The tendency for children to assume that word labels that apply to a particular object will also apply to similar objects

   g. Phonemes

8. Grammatical rules of a particular language that are important in the expression of novel ideas and fine gradations of meaning

   h. Semantics

9. The smallest units of meaning in a language that cannot be broken into any smaller parts that have meaning

   i. Inside-out theory

10. The aspect of language in which children learn to relate language to the physical and social context in which it is used in order to communicate effectively

    j. Underextensions

11. The theory of language development that proposes humans are born with innate brain mechanisms that are specific to language acquisition

    k. Learning theory

12. The theory of language development that proposes general cognitive abilities are sufficient to account for language acquisition

    l. Deictic words

13. The theory of language development that proposes humans acquire language by way of punishment, rewards, and imitation of models

    m. Taxonomic assumption

14. Word pair whose correct use requires considering the differing relations of objects to the speaker and the listener

    n. Whole-object assumption

MULTIPLE CHOICE QUESTIONS: Read the following questions and indicate your answer by marking the option that you think best answers each question.

1. Research on babbling has revealed that
   a. deaf children do not babble at any age.
   b. its frequency before the first birthday is a good predictor of later vocabulary.
   c. it begins in all infants around six months and increases in frequency until the age of one.
   d. all of the above are true.

2. Which of the following would be least likely to be included in a child's first words?
   a. names for toys or familiar objects in the home
   b. names for articles of clothing, animals, or body parts
   c. names for immovable objects such as a wall, table, or window
   d. names for people with whom the baby interacts

3. Studies that have investigated the speed of vocabulary development have revealed that
   a. girls begin to speak earlier than boys.
   b. variations are related partly to how much parents and other adults speak to the child.
   c. there are wide variations among children in word learning.
   d. all of the above are true.

4. The tendency for children to use an unfamiliar word to name an unfamiliar object is referred to as
   a. the taxonomic assumption.
   b. the novel name-nameless category principle.
   c. the whole-object assumption.
   d. the A- not B error.

5. The grammatical error, "I goed to the store," is due to which of the following phenomena?
   a. overregularization
   b. overextension
   c. underextension
   d. taxonomic assumption

6. Current research indicates that children begin to use "socialized" language and pragmatics
   a. much earlier than Piaget proposed.
   b. much later than Piaget proposed.
   c. not until the age of six or seven years.
   d. as indicated by both "b" and "c."

7. Research that has investigated early language development in children has revealed that
   a. most children can produce more words than they comprehend.
   b. most children can comprehend more words than they produce.
   c. males tend to acquire and use language significantly earlier than females.
   d. early babblers tend to acquire a larger vocabulary than late babblers by the school years.

8. The phenomenon of overregularization suggests that
   a. children appear to memorize lists of words but do not understand grammatical rules.
   b. children tend to define words too narrowly.
   c. children tend to define and apply words too broadly.
   d. children apply grammatical rules in language rather than merely memorize word lists.

9. Genie's failure to acquire language skills with the completeness of a preschool child provides partial support for
   a. the "critical-period" hypothesis.
   b. learning theory.
   c. the whole-object assumption.
   d. the taxonomic assumption.

10. The "inside-out" view of language acquisition is the belief that
    a. language is acquired by way of reinforcement, punishment, and imitation of models.
    b. children have innate brain mechanisms that specialize in language development.
    c. basic cognitive abilities are sufficient for language acquisition and development.
    d. language is not affected by "critical periods" of development.

TRUE AND FALSE QUESTIONS: Read the following statements and indicate whether you think each statement is true or false.

1. Research indicates that infants are unable to discriminate between similar phonemes until the age of six months.

2. If a particular phonemic discrimination is not part of an infant's language, the infant will lose the ability to make that discrimination.

3. Research has revealed that patterns of babbling are the same in deaf infants as they are in hearing infants.

4. In early language development, children tend to comprehend more words than they can produce.

5. The frequency of babbling in the first year accurately predicts how early or late normal children will begin to speak and the size of their vocabulary when they enter school.

6. Piaget's belief that children are not capable of "socialized" speech until the age of six or seven has been supported by current research.

7. Genie's failure to fully develop her language skills provides partial support for the critical-period hypothesis.

8. A number of studies provide evidence that child-directed language may facilitate early language development.

9. Children speak their first meaningful words sometime around their first birthday.

10. Most developmental psychologists believe that reinforcement, punishment, and imitation of models fully explain language acquisition.

FILL-IN-THE-BLANKS: Read the following sentences and write the missing word or words in the space provided.

1. The basic sound units that are combined to make words are called _____, of which there are approximately _____ in the English language.

2. The term _____ refers to the meaning system of a language and the term _____ refers to the grammatical rules that apply to a particular language.

3. It is important to remember that overextensions often occur in the _____ of speech but not in the _____ of speech.

4. An _____ is a word that can stand alone, and a _____ cannot stand alone but is always a part of a word.

5. Errors in which the use of a word is too broad or general are called _____ and errors in which the use of a word is too narrow are called _____.

6. In order to communicate effectively, children must learn to relate language to the _____ and _____ context in which it is used, an aspect of language called pragmatics.

7. The tendency for children to label unfamiliar objects with unfamiliar names is referred to as the _____ principle, and the tendency for children to assume that word labels that apply to a particular object will also apply to similar objects is referred to as the _____ principle.

8. The inside-out theorists believe that children are born with _____ brain mechanisms specific to language acquisition, whereas the outside-in theorists believe that _____ are sufficient to account for language learning.

9. Support for the nativist view of language comes from evidence that suggests there is a _____ for language development, after which language acquisition may be difficult if not impossible.

10. The tendency for adults to modify their speech when talking to infants, e.g., raising the pitch of the voice and exaggerating intonation, is referred to as _____ language.

MIX-AND-MATCH

1.	g	2.	h
3.	b	4.	j
5.	a	6.	n
7.	m	8.	e
9.	f	10.	c
11.	i	12.	d
13.	k	14.	l

MULTIPLE CHOICE

1.	c	2.	c
3.	d	4.	b
5.	a	6.	a
7.	b	8.	d
9.	a	10.	b

TRUE AND FALSE

1.	false	2.	true
3.	false	4.	true
5.	false	6.	false
7.	true	8.	true
9.	true	10.	false

FILL-IN-THE-BLANKS

1. phonemes; 40
2. semantics; syntax
3. production; comprehension
4. unbound morpheme; bound morpheme
5. overextensions; underextensions
6. social; physical;
7. novel name-nameless category; taxonomic assumption
8. innate; general cognitive abilities
9. critical period
10. child-directed

CHAPTER 9:
COGNITIVE DEVELOPMENT IN CHILDHOOD

CHAPTER OVERVIEW

As children grow older and mature, their cognitive abilities become more sophisticated. According to Piaget, thinking during the preoperational stage tends to be inflexible, incapable of reversibility, dominated by perceptual appearance, and incapable of considering more than one aspect of a situation at a time. However, as children enter into the stage of concrete operations, thinking becomes more flexible and they are capable of mental operations that are reversible. Children are also capable of decentration, i.e., the ability to focus on several aspects of an object or event at a time. Finally, thinking becomes less dependent on perceptual information and more logical during this period. According to Piaget, the transition from preoperational to concrete thinking is largely under the influence of biological and maturational influences.

Piaget's theory was based on carefully designed experiments that compared thinking and reasoning processes among children of various ages. Using various methods that tested children's "conservation" and "seriation" skills, Piaget was able to document differences in operations related to reversibility, decentration, seriation, transitive reasoning, class inclusion, and logical thinking between preoperational and concrete operational children. Several aspects of Piaget's original research have been challenged by researchers, however. For example, studies have shown that teaching can improve performance on conservation tasks and other types of "concrete" skills in preoperational children. More recent research also has revealed that preoperational children do better on tests measuring conservation skills, class inclusion, and spatial egocentrism than Piaget reported. Many experts believe that Piaget's tasks were too complex and his questions worded too abstractly for children to understand. Moreover, studies reveal that preoperational children are able to use a principle even though they are unable to explain the principle. Despite some of its theoretical and methodological flaws, Piaget's theory remains one the most influential theories in developmental psychology.

Information-processesing offers another view that differs from Piaget's theory. According to this view, thinking is information processing and is continuous rather than discontinuous. This tradition rejects the idea of cross-task generalities and focuses instead on the way in which task variation affects cognitive processing. Like Piaget, research in this area has found that children's use of rules becomes more sophisticated as they get older. However, these theorists view changes in the use of rules as incremental rather than stage-dependent. Information-processing theorists also maintain that developmental change such as selective attention may be due more to an accumulation of experience than to maturational processes. Finally, this perspective places greater emphasis on the importance of memory processes, which improve with age. Despite the valuable information provided by research in this area, information-processing models have been criticized for being too "static" in their view of cognitive development.

Developmental theorists also have been interested in determining the extent to which cognitive development is domain-specific. Children gain a fuller understanding of the way the mind operates as they grow older and develop empathy, perspective, and clearer distinctions between appearance and reality. Humans also appear to have some understanding of numbers as early as infancy, although numerical skills, such as counting, do not develop until the preschool years. Later, children develop more sophisticated skills that allow them to engage in numerical operations, such as addition and subtraction. Similarly, children's spatial abilities also undergo developmental changes as they grow older. An important contribution to cognitive theory is the Vygotskyan approach, which stresses the importance of environmental and social influences on cognitive processing. Despite their differences, most theorists agree that cognitive development is an active and constructive process, although controversy regarding its innate origins continues.

CHAPTER OUTLINE: Use the outline provided below by writing information related to each topic in the margins of the outline, e.g., definitions of terms and elaboration of concepts.

I. Piaget's Description

A. *Preoperational thought*

B. *The stage of concrete operations*

C. *Conservation, seriation, and class inclusion*

II. Questions about Piaget's theory

A. *Can cognitive development be accelerated?*

B. *Can preschoolers show concrete operational abilities?*

C. *Conservation of number, class inclusion, and spatial egocentrism*

D. *Why the new findings?*

E. *Evaluation of Piaget's theory*

III. Information-Processing Research on Cognitive Development

A. *The general approach*

B. *Information-processing analysis of particular tasks*

C. *Development of selective attention*

D. *Memory development and metamemory processes*

E. *Evaluation of the information-processing approach*

IV. Domain-Specific Research on Cognitive Development

A. *Theory of mind*

B. *Understanding of number*

C. *Spatial representation*

V. The Vygotskyan Approach to Cognitive Development

A. *The role of environment and culture*

VI. An Emerging New View

KEY DEFINITIONS AND TERMS: Define the following concepts and terms Try to provide an example for each word or term you have defined to help clarify its meaning.

Preoperational thought:

Concrete operational thought:

Operation:

Decentration:

The identity principle:

The equivalence principle:

Conservation:

Conservation of substance:

Conservation of number:

Seriation:

Reversibility:

Transitivity:

Class inclusion:

Principle of multiplication of classes or relations:

Spatial egocentrism:

Horizontal décalage:

Information-processing approach:

Selective attention:

Sensory memory:

Short-term memory:

Long-term memory:

Long-term memory retrieval:

Metamemory:

Domain-specific cognition:

The Vygotskyan approach:

Setting the menu:

Zone of proximal development:

REVIEW QUESTIONS: Below are questions that relate to key concepts and information covered in your textbook. Answer the questions as thoroughly and completely as possible. Try to provide examples to support your answer and to clarify meaning.

1. According to Piaget, how do preoperational and concrete operational children differ in their cognitive abilities?

2. Describe the stage of concrete operations. What are some of the cognitive abilities that children acquire in this stage? Describe the research methods used by Piaget to test children's "conservation" skills, their seriation and transitive reasoning skills, and their understanding of class inclusion.

3. Can cognitive development be accelerated? Discuss the research that has investigated preschoolers' concrete operational abilities. Are they capable of conservation of number, class inclusion, and taking the perspective of others? Why has current research reported findings that differ from Piaget's original research findings?

4. Is cognitive development domain general or domain specific? Does research indicate that development occurs in stages as proposed by Piaget? How did Piaget attempt to explain the fact that some children were capable of seriation tasks but failed conservation tasks?

5. Describe the information-processing approach in the study of cognitive development. What are some of the important ways in which this view differs from Piaget's theory?

6. Describe the research by Robert Siegler that has analyzed the age changes in the rules children use to make judgments about certain problems. How do the rules that children use to the "teeter-totter" task differ as they get older? How does Siegler differ from Piaget in his theoretical interpretation of his research findings?

7. Describe research that investigated the development of selective attention. How does the information-processing perspective explain the changes that occur in children's selective attention as they get older?

8. Describe the three basic types of memory that psychologists have identified and the developmental changes that occur in each of these memory systems. To what does the term "metamemory" refer, and in what way do metamemory skills change with age?

9. Evaluate information-processing's approach in the study of cognitive development. What are its strengths and weaknesses? What are some of its limitations?

10. Describe some of the ways in which children develop a theory of mind. What are some of the cognitive skills that provide children with a better understanding of other people's minds and their workings, and when do these skills emerge? By what age can most children distinguish appearance from reality?

11. Describe the developmental changes that affect children's understanding of numbers. At what age do children first appear to have some sense of numbers? How do children's capacity for understanding numbers change as they get older?

12. Describe the developmental changes that affect children's understanding of spatial representation. At what age do children first indicate a capacity for spatial relations, e.g., the ability to locate hidden objects? What type of developmental changes in spatial understanding occur as children get older?

13. Describe the Vygotskyan approach to cognitive development. How do adults arrange the context within which children learn and guide children in exploring those contexts? Discuss three ways in which culture is crucial to cognitive development.

14. Discuss the way in which various approaches and theories of cognitive development have converged over the past several years. What are some issues on which cognitive theorists agree and disagree?

MIX-AND-MATCH: In the left-hand column below are some key concepts or definitions. Choose the term from the column on the right that best matches each definition provided in the column on the left.

1. According to Piaget's theory, the stage of cognitive development in which children's thinking is egocentric, inflexible, and incapable of reversibility

   a. Seriation

2. According to Piaget's theory, the stage of cognitive development in which children first engage in mental operations that have reversibility and are capable of decentration

   b. Short-term memory

3. The ability to arrange objects according to some quantified dimension, such as weight or size

   c. Vygotskyan approach

4. The principle of logic which states that there are certain fixed relationships among the qualities of objects

   d. Long-term memory

5. The principle of logic in which children understand that there are hierarchical relations among categories

   e. Operation

6. The inability of an individual to understand another person's perspective

   f. Information-processing

7. Type of memory that is briefest, lasting no longer than a second or two unless stored

   g. Metamemory

8. Type of memory that holds information for only about 30 seconds unless an effort is made to retain it

   h. Spatial egocentrism

9. Type of memory that is potentially available for a long time, perhaps forever

   i. Transitivity

10. Type of memory process in which individuals have some knowledge of how their memory systems work and how to make them work better

    j. Preoperational stage

11. Theoretical approach in the study of cognition that is interested in how the human mind represents and manipulates information

    k. Sensory memory

12. Theoretical approach which stresses the importance of environmental and social influences on cognitive processing and the role that adults have in arranging the contexts in which children learn

    l. Class inclusion

13. A term used by Piaget to describe a basic cognitive structure that is used to transform information

    m. Concrete operational stage

MULTIPLE CHOICE QUESTIONS: Read the following questions and indicate your answer by marking the option that you think best answers each question.

1. Which of the following is <u>not</u> true about children in the preoperational stage?
   a. Their thinking tends to be egocentric.
   b. They are capable of mental operations that are reversible.
   c. Their thinking tends to be dominated by perceptual appearances.
   d. They are incapable of focusing on more than one aspect of a situation at a time.

2. The principle which states that basic attributes of an object do not change is referred to as
   a. decentration.
   b. the identity principle.
   c. the equivalence principle.
   d. reversibility.

3. According to Piaget, a four-year-old who believes that there is more water if it is poured from a short container than one that is tall and narrow has not grasped the principle of
   a. seriation.
   b. transitivity.
   c. conservation of number.
   d. conservation of substance.

4. Eight-year-old Jason can arrange sticks of different lengths in order from shortest to longest. According to Piaget, Jason is capable of which of the following operations?
   a. seriation
   b. class inclusion
   c. decentration
   d. conservation of number

5. Current research indicates that preschool children can take other people's perspective
   a. much earlier than Piaget proposed.
   b. by at least the age of two.
   c. no earlier than the age of five.
   d. as proposed in both "a" and "b."

6. Information-processing theorists believe that
   a. children's cognitive abilities are controlled by maturational factors.
   b. children's cognitive abilities develop in age-related stages.
   c. developmental stages are gradual and continuous rather than discontinuous.
   d. both "a" and "b" are true.

7. Siegler's research on rule use found that most people use _____ by age 17.
   a. rule one exclusively
   b. rules two or three
   c. rule three
   d. rule four

8. Which of the following is <u>not</u> an information-processing explanation as to why children's selective attention improves as they get older?
   a. Children become better able to control the deployment of attention as they get older.
   b. Children's attentional patterns become more adaptive to the situation as they get older.
   c. Children become more able to plan ahead as they get older.
   d. Children's brains become more biologically mature as they get older.

9. Most children are able to distinguish appearance from reality by the age of
   a. two years.
   b. three years.
   c. four years.
   d. five years.

10. The notion that social and cultural factors influence cognitive development is central to
   a. the information-processing approach.
   b. the Vygotskyan approach.
   c. the biological approach.
   d. the Siegler approach.

TRUE AND FALSE QUESTIONS: Read the following statements and indicate whether you think each statement is true or false.

1. Seriation refers to a child's ability to focus on more than one aspect of a situation at a time.

2. Research that has tested some of Piaget's theory has revealed that cognitive development cannot be accelerated by teaching or training.

3. Studies indicate that children are able to take the perspective of someone else as early as the age of two.

4. Studies indicate that children's cognitive abilities tend to be "domain specific," e.g., they may succeed at seriation but fail at conservation.

5. Information-processing theory proposes that developmental change is discontinuous and qualitative.

6. Siegler's research on rules revealed that 90 percent of the subjects who were tested used rule four by the age of 17.

7. The type of memory that is briefest in duration, lasting no more than a few seconds, is short-term memory.

8. Children clearly understand that other people may act on their own beliefs, even when those differ from those of other people, by the age of three years.

9. Infants can distinguish one object from two and two objects from three as early as four months old.

10. Studies indicate that children cannot solve addition and subtraction problems presented nonverbally until at least the age of three.

FILL-IN-THE-BLANKS: Read the following sentences and write the missing word or words in the space provided.

1. Piaget used the "three mountains task" to demonstrate _____, a perspective which most children have until after the age of _____ years.

2. Unlike preoperational children, Piaget proposed that children in the concrete operation stage can engage in mental operations that have _____; that they are capable of _____, i.e., are able to focus on several attributes of an object at one time; and that they shift from relying on _____ information to using _____ principles.

3. Studies in which children are asked if the amount of liquid changes when poured into a container with a different size and shape are demonstrating _____. Studies in which children are asked if the quantity of buttons changes when the buttons are spaced farther apart are demonstrating _____.

4. The ability to arrange objects according to some quantified dimension, such as weight or size, is called _____. The logical principle which states that there are certain fixed relationships among the qualities of objects is called _____.

5. The logical principle that there are hierarchal relations among categories is called _____. The idea that objects can belong to more than one category or more than one relationship at any time is a principle called _____.

6. Research by Siegler has revealed that _____ percent of children's performance in problem solving can be successfully categorized as using one or another of four rules. Most 5-year-olds use rule _____, most 9-year-olds use rules _____ and _____ and most 13- to 17-year-olds use rule _____.

7. Memory that holds information for a maximum of 30 seconds unless an effort is made to retain it is called _____. The knowledge of how memory systems work and how to make them work better is referred to as _____.

8. The Vygotskyan approach stresses the importance of the _____ environment and the role of _____ in cognitive development. Vygotsky described an adult's structuring of the child's interaction with the world as fostering growth in the _____.

9. Studies reveal that preschool children have been found to use _____ even when they don't count exactly correctly according to adult standards.

10. Studies indicate that the cognitive development of preoperational children can be _____ to the concrete operational stage if they are provided with _____ on basic cognitive skills such as conservation.

ANSWERS TO PRACTICE TEST ITEMS

MIX-AND-MATCH

1.	j	2.	m
3.	a	4.	i
5.	l	6.	h
7.	k	8.	b
9.	d	10.	g
11.	f	12.	c
13.	e		

MULTIPLE CHOICE

1.	b	2.	b
3.	d	4.	a
5.	d	6.	c
7.	c	8.	d
9.	d	10.	b

TRUE AND FALSE

1.	false	2.	false
3.	true	4.	true
5.	false	6.	false
7.	false	8.	true
9.	true	10.	true

FILL-IN-THE-BLANKS

1. spatial egocentrism; six
2. reversibility; decentration; perceptual; logical
3. conservation of substance; conservation of number
4. seriation; transitivity
5. class inclusion; multiplication of classes or relations
6. 90; one; two or three; three
7. short-term; metamemory
8. social; culture; zone of proximal development
9. counting principles
10. accelerated; training or teaching

CHAPTER OVERVIEW

Intelligence is defined as the capacity to learn and use the skills that are needed for successful adaptation to one's environment and culture. A long-standing debate is whether intelligence is a general or specific trait. Although many experts agree that there are several types of intelligence, not all agree on what those abilities are. Some experts emphasize verbal and math abilities, whereas others emphasize cognitive processes such as memory and problem solving.

There are several theories of intelligence. Horn proposes that individuals have "crystallized" abilities, which represent an accumulation of knowledge, and "fluid" abilities, which are used in the analysis of information and problem solving. Gardner proposes that there are six types of intelligence and that individuals can be proficient in some areas and deficient in other areas. Sternberg proposes that intelligence has three components, consisting of cognitive process and knowledge, rapidity of learning, and the ability to adapt to one's cultural and social environment.

Although earlier tests only provided a "general" intelligence score, more current tests provide scores on several dimensions of intelligence. It is important to recognize that although IQ scores may reflect innate abilities, they also are influenced by environmental factors and an individual's opportunity to learn. Factors such as motivation, fatigue, and attention span can affect IQ scores by several points. Moreover, the IQ scores of children may show significant changes as they grow older, with increases averaging 28.5 points. Finally, it is important to acknowledge that although individuals who perform well on measures of intelligence are usually competent, it cannot be assumed that individuals who do not perform well are not competent.

Psychologists also have been interested in identifying the factors that determine achievement motivation. Studies reveal that achievement motivation is affected by children's attainment value, their standards of performance, their expectations and beliefs about their own abilities, and how they attribute their successes and failures. As children grow older, their expectations become more realistic, they use social comparisons more frequently, they set higher levels of aspiration, and they also tend to show more test anxiety which can negatively affect performance. Fortunately, training may alleviate test anxiety and improve children's academic performance.

Research has investigated whether there are group differences in intelligence and motivation. Studies reveal that girls tend to have superior verbal abilities, but the differences usually fade after the age of two years. Studies have also revealed that Chinese and Japanese children perform better than American children in math and some reading skills, although they do not differ in general intellectual abilities. Differences in black and white IQ scores also have been reported. However, research indicates that social and cultural factors play an important role in achievement and intelligence. For example, a longitudinal study revealed that a mother's education and social status were better predictors of IQ than prenatal history or infant intelligence tests. Researchers also make the distinction between intellectual differences and intellectual deficits and have attempted to construct IQ tests that are not culturally biased.

Studies reveal that the home environment, affectionate involvement between parent and child, parenting styles, and parents' teaching behavior significantly affect IQ and achievement motivation. Programs such as Head Start have shown that early intervention has significant and long-term effects on children's intellectual development. Studies also reveal that intervention in infancy as well as educational television programs can significantly improve the IQ scores of high-risk children. Recognizing the interplay between the individual and the environment is vital to a better understanding of children's intellectual development and achievement motivation.

CHAPTER OUTLINE: Use the outline provided below by writing information related to each topic in the margins of the outline, e.g., definitions of terms and elaboration of concepts.

I. Defining and Conceptualizing Intelligence

A. *One ability or more?*

B. *The dimensions of intelligence*

C. *Early efforts to measure intelligence*

D. *Tests based on cognitive processes*

E. *Limitations on measures of IQ*

F. *How should IQ be tested?*

II. Motivation and School Achievement

A. *Determinants of achievement motivation*

B. *Changing attributions and achievement behavior*

C. *Developmental patterns in achievement motivation*

D. *Test anxiety*

III. Group Differences in Intelligence and Achievement

A. *Sex differences*

B. *Social class and ethnic group differences*

C. *Differences vs. deficits*

IV. Individual Differences in Intelligence and Achievement

A. *The home environment*

B. *Affection and involvement with the child*

C. *Parental beliefs, expectations, and values*

D. *Parenting styles and discipline*

E. *Parents' teaching behavior*

F. *Early intervention*

G. *Interaction between constitution and environment*

KEY DEFINITIONS AND TERMS: Define the following concepts and terms Try to provide an example for each word or term you have defined to help clarify its meaning.

Intelligence:

Fluid abilities:

Crystallized abilities:

Aptitude:

Achievement:

Attainment value:

Standards of performance:

Autonomous standards:

Social-comparison standards:

Perceived self-efficacy:

Internal vs. external attributions:

Stable vs. unstable attributions:

Learned helplessness:

REVIEW QUESTIONS: Below are questions that relate to key concepts and information covered in your textbook. Answer the questions as thoroughly and completely as possible. Try to provide examples to support your answer and to clarify meaning.

1. How is intelligence typically defined? Discuss the way in which social and cultural factors might affect the way in which intelligence is defined and measured.

2. Describe the following conceptualizations of intelligence: Horn's "crystallized" vs. "fluid" abilities, Gardner's multiple intelligences and Sternberg's triarchic theory. How do these conceptualizations of intelligence differ from each other?

3. Describe the history of intelligence testing. How have scales that measure intelligence changed since Binet first introduced his test in the early 1900s? Do most current tests provide only one general score or do they include subtests that provide scores for different abilities?

4. Discuss the limitations on measures of IQ. What are some of the factors that can influence scores on intelligence tests? Is IQ innate and "fixed" for life? Do longitudinal studies suggest that intelligence changes as children get older, or do they suggest that it remains relatively stable throughout life? Support your answer with relevant studies.

5. What is the difference between aptitude and achievement? Do intelligence tests measure both? Does performance on an IQ test reflect an individual's competence? Discuss.

6. Is achievement motivation a "general" trait or does it vary across tasks and situations? Discuss the way in which attainment value and standards of performance influence a child's level of achievement motivation.

7. Discuss the way in which expectancies and beliefs about various abilities can affect children's performance. Discuss the way in which children's attributions of their successes and failures can affect their level of motivation.

8. Discuss some of the strategies that have been used to change attributional patterns and achievement behavior in children.

9. Discuss the way in which perceptions of self-efficacy, attributions and attainment values change throughout childhood.

10. What are some of the causes of test anxiety and how can test anxiety affect academic performance? Discuss some of the ways of reducing the negative effects of test anxiety.

11. Discuss some of the sex differences in academic skills that have been reported. In general, do gender differences in verbal and spatial abilities tend to be large or small? Discuss the way in which expectations, cultural factors and attributional patterns might affect the academic performance of males and females. Can different tasks measure different aspects of the same ability, e.g., spatial ability?

12. Discuss the research that has made cross-national comparisons of intellectual abilities. How does the intellectual performance of American children compare to Chinese and Japanese children? Do the differences appear to be genetically or culturally based?

13. Discuss the research that has made within-country comparisons of intellectual abilities. What IQ differences between black and white children have been reported? Does the available evidence suggest that the differences are due to genetic factors or environmental factors? Cite relevant studies to support your answer.

14. Discuss the difference vs. deficit approach in explaining IQ differences. Discuss the way in which test bias can affect measurements of intelligence. Is it legal in some states to use IQ tests to identify and place children in "special" classes?

15. Discuss the ways in which the following factors can influence intellectual development and achievement motivation: the home environment, affection and involvement with the child, parental beliefs, expectations and values, parenting styles, and parental teaching behavior.

16. Discuss the way in which early intervention programs, such as Head Start, can facilitate intellectual development and achievement motivation. What did early evaluations of Head Start programs reveal? What is the current status of early intervention programs? Do they make a significant difference?

17. Discuss research that has investigated intervention in infancy. Do high-risk children benefit from early intervention? Discuss the positive effects that intervention with television programs such as *Sesame Street* can have on the intellectual development of high-risk children.

18. Discuss the way in which a child's constitution and the environment interact and influence intellectual development. Describe Horowitz's "continuum" model and the way in which it can be applied to understanding particular aspects of children's intellectual development.

MIX-AND-MATCH: In the left-hand column below are some key concepts or definitions. Choose the term from the column on the right that best matches each definition provided in the column on the left.

1. The capacity to learn and use the skills that are required for successful adaptation to the demands of one's culture and environment

    a. Attributions

2. Intellectual abilities that refer to the knowledge a person has accumulated

    b. Aptitude

3. Intellectual abilities that refer to the processes individuals use when solving problems and dealing with new information

    c. Sternberg's triarchic theory

4. The ability to learn a new skill or to do well in some future learning situation

    d. Achievement motivation

5. Term used to describe how much a person has learned in a particular course or school subject

    e. Fluid abilities

6. An overall tendency to evaluate one's performance against standards of excellence, to strive for successful performance, and to experience pleasure contingent on successful performance

    f. Intelligence

7. Standards individuals adopt that are personal or are based on comparisons with their own past performance

    g. Perceived self-efficacy

8. Standards that are based on comparisons with other people's performances

    h. Crystallized abilities

9. A self-concept of ability that is concerned with judgments of how well one can execute the course of action required to deal with prospective situations

    i. Achievement

10. Inferences that individuals make about the causes of their own or another's behavior

    j. Social-comparison standards

11. Pattern of maladaptive attributions in which individuals come to believe that their successes don't reflect ability and that their failures cannot be reversed by effort

    k. Gardner's Multiple Intelligences

12. Theory which proposes that intelligence is comprised of linguistic, musical, logical-mathematical, spatial, bodily-kinesthetic, and personal intelligences

    l. Autonomous standards

13. Theory which proposes that intelligence is comprised of cognitive processes and knowledge, rapidity of learning, and the ability to adapt to one's social and cultural environment

    m. Learned helplessness

MULTIPLE CHOICE QUESTIONS: Read the following questions and indicate your answer by marking the option that you think best answers each question.

1. Which of the following is <u>not</u> one of the domains of intelligence included in Sternberg's triarchic theory of intelligence?
   a. cognitive processes and knowledge
   b. how rapidly an individual learns
   c. linguistic intelligence
   d. adaptation to one's social and cultural environment

2. The original Stanford-Binet intelligence test
   a. was the first to provide a multidimensional assessment of intelligence.
   b. was designed to keep mentally inferior people from migrating to the United States.
   c. provided only a single score - it was assumed intelligence was a generalized quality.
   d. incorporated both "a" and "b."

3. Most experts agree that
   a. an IQ score is a pure index of innate potential in an individual.
   b. IQ is fixed for life by the age of three.
   c. IQ scores often show significant increases as children grow older.
   d. as children grow older, their IQ scores become poorer predictors of later performance.

4. Children who are most likely to expect future failure are those who tend to attribute past failures to
   a. internal and stable causes.
   b. external and unstable causes.
   c. external and stable causes.
   d. internal and unstable causes.

5. Which of the following is <u>not</u> a developmental change that occurs as children grow older?
   a. Their expectancies about their abilities and performance become more realistic.
   b. They are less likely to use social comparisons in evaluating their own performance.
   c. They set higher levels of aspiration for themselves, e.g., choose more difficult tasks.
   d. They express more anxiety about failure, i.e, test anxiety.

6. Research that has investigated differences in intelligence between males and females has revealed that
   a.. boys tend to have slightly higher IQs in the early years than girls.
   b. males tend to be intellectually superior to females by adulthood.
   c. girls tend to be verbally superior to boys, but the differences fade after the age of two.
   d. males are better at math than females in the elementary school years.

7. Cross-national comparisons of Asian and American students have revealed that
   a. Asian students are superior in their general intellectual ability.
   b. Asian students perform better in mathematics and some reading skills.
   c. Asian students perform better in math and some reading, but not in general intelligence.
   d. both "a" and "b" are true.

8. Research has revealed that children with high IQs and achievement levels have mothers
   a. who are affectionate and verbally responsive to them.
   b. who have irregular and unpredictable routines.
   c. who are strict with their children.
   d. who exhibit both "b" and "c."

9. Achievement motivation in school has been associated with which of the following parenting styles?
   a. authoritative parenting
   b. authoritarian parenting
   c. permissive parenting
   d. rejecting-neglecting parenting

10. Well-controlled studies of early intervention programs such as Head Start have revealed that they
    a. do not significantly affect children's academic performance.
    b. benefit middle-income children but not lower-income children.
    c. produce lasting benefits for economically disadvantaged children.
    d. produce lasting benefits for economically disadvantaged girls but not for boys.

TRUE AND FALSE QUESTIONS: Read the following statements and indicate whether you think each statement is true or false.

1. Longitudinal studies reveal that IQ scores do not change significantly as children grow older and that IQ is usually "fixed" by the age of two.

2. The early Stanford-Binet test provided only a summary IQ score because it was assumed that intelligence was a generalized quality.

3. Research has revealed that males of all ages score significantly higher on intelligence tests than females.

4. Children who have the least amount of achievement motivation are those who tend to attribute past failures to stable causes.

5. Studies indicate that across a wide range of achievement areas, boys often have higher expectancies than girls, even when their average past performance is similar or lower.

6. Chinese and Japanese children score significantly higher than American children on various tests of general intellectual ability.

7. Children with the highest level of achievement motivation come from families who use authoritative parenting styles.

8. It is currently against the law in all states to use IQ scores to place children in "special" classes.

9. Studies reveal that students' expectancies of success are more closely related to their parents' expectancies than to their own past performance.

10. Early intervention programs such as Head Start do not appear to have a significant effect on the academic performance of high-risk children.

FILL-IN-THE-BLANKS: Read the following sentences and write the missing word or words in the space provided.

1. According to Horn, _____ abilities refer to the knowledge that a person has accumulated and _____ abilities refer to the processes individuals use in problem solving and dealing with new information.

2. Gardner suggests that six candidates for multiple intelligences are _____ intelligence; _____ intelligence;_____ intelligence; _____ intelligence; _____ intelligence and _____ intelligence.

3. According to Sternberg's triarchic theory, the three components of intelligence are _____, _____ and the ability to adapt to one's _____ and _____ environment.

4. The term _____ refers to the ability to learn a new skill or to do well in some future learning situation whereas _____ describes how much a person has learned in a particular course or school subject.

5. The concept individuals have about their ability and how well they can execute courses of action required to deal with prospective situations is called _____.

6. Inferences about the causes of one's own or someone else's behavior are called _____. A pattern of maladaptive attributions in which individuals come to believe that their successes do not reflect ability and that their failures cannot be reversed by effort has been labeled _____.

7. During the first few years of school, children's stated expectancies become more _____, they increasingly use _____ in evaluating their own performance, they set higher levels of _____ for themselves and they express more _____ about test failure.

8. Males are more likely to show adaptive attributions, i.e., they tend to attribute their successes to _____ and their failures to _____.

9. The assumption that minority and lower-class children have deficient intelligence is sometimes called the _____ model. It is more accurate to say that nonwhite and lower-class children often learn _____ skills.

10. One implication of the "difference" model is that tests of intelligence are _____ against lower-class and minority children.

ANSWERS TO PRACTICE TEST ITEMS

MIX-AND-MATCH

1.	f	2.	h
3.	e	4.	b
5.	i	6.	d
7.	l	8.	j
9.	g	10.	a
11.	m	12.	k
13.	c		

MULTIPLE CHOICE

1.	c	2.	c
3.	c	4.	a
5.	b	6.	c
7.	c	8.	a
9.	a	10.	c

TRUE AND FALSE

1.	false	2.	true
3.	false	4.	true
5.	true	6.	false
7.	true	8.	false
9.	true	10.	false

FILL-IN-THE-BLANKS

1. crystallized; fluid
2. linguistic; musical; logical-mathematical; spatial; bodily-kinesthetic; personal
3. cognitive processes and knowledge; how rapidly individuals learn; social and cultural
4. aptitude; achievement
5. perceived self-efficacy
6. attributions; learned helplessness
7. realistic; social comparison; aspiration; anxiety
8. ability; luck
9. deficit; different
10. biased

CHAPTER 11:
DEVELOPMENT OF SOCIAL BEHAVIOR IN CHILDHOOD

CHAPTER OVERVIEW

The self-concept is often measured by having individuals describe themselves. As children grow older, their self-descriptions are less likely to include physical traits and more likely to include psychological traits and abstract statements. Studies also reveal that measures of self-esteem tend to be less positive as children grow older. Adults may facilitate a positive self-esteem by emphasizing their children's competencies and strengths.

Self-control tends to improve as children grow older. Studies reveal that children who are able to delay immediate gratification tend to be more responsible and mature, higher in achievement motivation, more intelligent and better students than other children. Children can be trained to delay gratification by learning to not think about the desired object, through self-instruction, by monitoring themselves to resist distraction, through positive labeling and by observing a model who delays gratification. Although the development of self-control is important, extreme behavior in either direction may be maladaptive. Children who are overcontrollers tend to be conforming and overly rigid in their delay of gratification, whereas undercontrollers tend to be spontaneous and nonconforming but unable to delay gratification. Ego-resilient children have a more adaptive pattern of behavior, exercising control in some situations and flexibility in other situations. Studies reveal that children high in ego control and resilience tend to be better adjusted than children who are low in ego control and resilience.

The four features of sex typing that are important to the self-concept are gender identity, sex role identity, sex role preference, and sex role adoption. Kohlberg suggested that children who have already developed a gender identity actively seek information appropriate to their gender and act accordingly. Mischel argues that sex typing is learned through operant conditioning and observation of role models. Schema theorists propose that children interpret events according to their gender schemata. According to this view, children for whom gender is particularly salient show stronger sex typing. Androgynous individuals have a mixture of both masculine and feminine traits. Teaching children that gender is biological, and that genitals not behavior, define a person's sex, and placing less emphasis on gender as a category can reduce rigid sex typing.

Another important component of children's self-concept is their racial identity. Most children classify people according to skin color by age three, although minority children become aware of ethnic differences at an earlier age. A survey of black adolescents revealed that 95 percent mentioned their race when asked the question "who are you," indicating that race is a salient feature in the self-concept of African Americans. Past research has revealed lower self-esteems and more negative attitudes toward their race among black children than white children. Current studies are contradictory, revealing both positive and negative group attitudes. The contradictions may be due to differences in group versus personal identity. Moreover, social and political changes also may account for more current positive attitudes among African Americans.

Researchers have been interested in the development of prosocial and aggressive behavior in children. Studies on prosocial behavior have revealed that it is fairly stable over time and varies according to culture. Prosocial behavior also is related to children's level of empathy and experiences in role taking. Studies have shown that modeling, induction and encouraging responsibility can facilitate prosocial behavior in children. Longitudinal studies reveal that aggressive behavior also appears to be stable over time. In all social classes and cultures, males are more aggressive than females. Biological factors, such as testosterone levels and temperament, account for some of the differences. However, social factors, such as parenting styles and use of physical punishment, are also important determinants of aggression.

CHAPTER OUTLINE: Use the outline provided below by writing information related to each topic in the margins of the outline, e.g., definitions of terms and elaboration of concepts.

I. **Developing a Sense of Self**

    A. *Self-concept*

    B. *Self-esteem*

    C. *Self-control*

    D. *Developing self-control*

    E. *Over- and undercontrol*

    F. *The gendered self*

    G. *The development of sex- yping*

    H. *The ethnic self*

II. **The Developing Self and Others**

    A. *Prosocial behavior*

    B. *Facilitating prosocial behavior*

    C. *Aggression*

    D. *Patterns of aggressive behavior*

    E. *Sex differences*

    F. *Determinants of aggression*

KEY DEFINITIONS AND TERMS: Define the following concepts and terms Try to provide an example for each word or term you have defined to help clarify its meaning.

Self-concept:

Self-esteem:

Self-control:

Ego control:

Overcontrollers:

Ego resilience:

Undercontrollers:

Sex typing:

Gender identity:

Sex role identity:

Sex role preferences:

Sex role adoption:

Gender constancy:

REVIEW QUESTIONS: Below are questions that relate to key concepts and information covered in your textbook. Answer the questions as thoroughly and completely as possible. Try to provide examples to support your answer and to clarify meaning.

1. Describe some of the ways children's self-concept and self-esteem change as they grow older. How does the Self-Perception Profile for Children measure self-esteem and how does it reduce response bias?

2. How did Freud and social learning theorists differ in their explanations of self-control? Describe methods that researchers have used to measure self-control. What are the traits of children who are able to delay gratification?

3. What are the factors that influence children's ability to delay gratification? Describe the training techniques that have been used to enhance children's ability to delay gratification.

4. Describe the personality differences and behavioral differences between "overcontrollers" and "undercontrollers." What specific combinations of "ego control" and "ego resilience" predict good adjustment in children by the age of seven? What specific combinations predict poor adjustment in children by the age of seven?

5. Describe the four features of sex typing and discuss the development of sex typing through childhood.

6. Discuss the theoretical explanations of sex typing in children proposed by Kohlberg, Mischel and schema theorists. Include research evidence that supports each view in your answer.

7. Discuss the research that has examined the role that ethnicity plays in children's self-concept. At what age can children classify people according to skin color? Describe research that indicates race is more salient for black children than for white children.

8. Compare the research findings on the self-esteem of black children conducted in the 1940s and 1950s to current research. How has the self-esteem of black children changed in the last 50 years? How can some of the apparent contradictions in current studies be explained? What are some of the social and historical factors that have contributed to changes in the self-esteem of black children?

9. Discuss the research that has studied prosocial behavior in children. Does there appear to be a general prosocial trait? Are prosocial tendencies in children stable over time? Are variations in prosocial behavior related to the culture in which children are raised? Support your answer with relevant research.

10. Discuss the research that has investigated the effects of modeling on prosocial behavior in children. How do "symbolic" modeling and "real" modeling differ in their effect on prosocial behavior? What has research revealed about the personal histories of people who are "unusually" altruistic?

11. Discuss the way in which induction can affect prosocial behavior. Do parents who use induction have children who tend to be more or less prosocial? Support your answer with relevant research.

12. Discuss the way in which patterns of aggressive behavior change as children grow older. Is aggression, regardless of its expression, stable over time? Describe the longitudinal study conducted by Huesmann and his colleagues. What did the findings of their study reveal?

13. Discuss the way in which children's cognition, interpretations of behavior, and information processing may contribute to the stability of aggression over time.

14. What has research revealed about gender differences in aggression? Are gender differences in aggression found only in some cultures and societies or do they appear to be universal?

15. What are some of the determinants of aggression that have been identified by researchers? Discuss the influence that biology, parenting styles, punishment, family interactions and socialization have on the development of aggression.

MIX-AND-MATCH: In the left-hand column below are some key concepts or definitions. Choose the term from the column on the right that best matches each definition provided in the column on the left.

1. Term used to refer to the assessment individuals have of their own attributes and abilities

2. The negative and positive values that individuals assign to their own attributes

3. The term used to describe children who show strong tendencies toward conformity, inhibition, undue delay of gratification and reluctance to explore new situations

4. Term used to describe children who are emotionally expressive and spontaneous, nonconforming and exploratory, but also distractable and unable to delay gratification

5. Term that refers to the key component underlying children who are overcontrollers or undercontrollers

6. An index of flexibility or adaptability that allows some children to be spontaneous and expressive in some situations and controlling in other situations

7. Term used to describe the ways in which biological gender and its cultural associations are incorporated into the child's self-perceptions and behavior

8. Term that refers to acceptance of one's basic biological nature as male or female, i.e., the fundamental sense of being a girl or a boy

9. Term that refers to the gender that a person values or would like to be

10. Acting in ways that are culturally defined as masculine or feminine

11. Term that refers to a child's understanding that gender does not change

12. Term that refers to a person who combines feminine psychological qualities with masculine attributes

13. Term that refers to positive social actions, including altruism, helping, sharing, caring, and sympathizing

14. Term that refers to a style of discipline in which parents reason with their children and point out the painful consequences of their misbehavior

a. Ego control

b. Sex role preference

c. Sex typing

d. Ego resilience

e. Self-concept

f. Prosocial behavior

g. Androgynous

h. Self-esteem

i. Gender constancy

j. Overcontrollers

k. Gender identity

l. Undercontrollers

m. Induction

n. Sex role adoption

MULTIPLE CHOICE QUESTIONS: Read the following questions and indicate your answer by marking the option that you think best answers each question.

1. During middle childhood, self-descriptions shift gradually to
   a. statements based more on physical attributes.
   b. more abstract statements.
   c. statements that describe favorite activities.
   d. statements incorporated by both "a" and "c."

2. Research that has studied self-esteem in children has found that
   a. self-esteem tends to improve as children grow older.
   b. self-esteem tends to worsen as children grow older.
   c. self-esteem does not usually change as children grow older.
   d. self-esteem improves for girls but worsens for boys.

3. According to Freud, self-control improves as children grow older because
   a. ego processes begin to exert more control and influence over behavior.
   b. the id begins to exert more control and influence over behavior.
   c. children develop a cognitive "schemata" that governs their behavior.
   d. children begin to observe and imitate the role models in their environment.

4. Which of the following was not cited as an effective strategy to improve children's self-control?
   a. Use "positive labeling" by telling children how patient they are.
   b. Teach children to monitor themselves so as to resist distraction.
   c. Punish children when they are unable to delay gratification and engage in self-control.
   d. Have children observe models who defer gratification.

5. Children who show the best social adjustment by age seven are those who combine
   a. high ego control and high ego resilience at age three.
   b. low ego control and low ego resilience at age three.
   c. high ego control and low ego resilience at age three.
   d. low ego control and high ego resilience at age three.

6. The fundamental sense of being a girl or a boy is referred to as
   a. sex role acceptance.
   b. gender identity.
   c. sex role identity.
   d. sex typing.

7. Most children develop a sense of gender constancy by the age of
   a. 18 months.
   b. two or three years.
   c. four years.
   d. five or six years.

8. A study asking the question, "Who are you?" revealed that _____ of the black adolescents surveyed mentioned being black or Negro in their self-description.
   a. 25 percent
   b. 50 percent
   c. 75 percent
   d. 95 percent

9. Longitudinal studies on prosocial behavior have revealed that
   a. variations in prosocial behavior are unrelated to the culture in which children grow up.
   c. prosocial tendencies do not remain stable over time.
   c. the relation between empathy and prosocial behavior increases with age.
   d. there does not appear to be a general "prosocial trait."

10. A longitudinal study conducted by Heusmann and his colleagues found that
   a. individuals who were aggressive at the age of eight years were three times more likely to have a criminal record by the age of 19 years than children who were not aggressive.
   b. individuals who were aggressive at the age of eight years were significantly more likely to be aggressive toward their spouses than children who were not aggressive.
   c. there were no significant differences in adult levels of aggression between individuals who had been rated aggressive or non-aggressive as children.
   d. both "a" and "b" are true.

TRUE AND FALSE QUESTIONS: Read the following statements and indicate whether you think each statement is true or false.

1. A study revealed that children who were overcontrollers at the age of three years were shy and inhibited at age seven.

2. Children who are high in ego control and ego resilience at the age of three years tend to be better adjusted by the age of seven than children who are low in ego control and ego resilience.

3. Children are able to classify people according to their skin color as early as the age of three years.

4. Studies indicate that ethnicity is a more salient feature of the self-concept for black children than for white children.

5. Minority children are aware of ethnic differences earlier than nonminority children.

6. Prosocial behavior is a general trait that tends to remain stable over time.

7. The relation between empathy and prosocial behavior tends to decrease with age.

8. Symbolic modeling significantly increases prosocial behavior in real-life situations.

9. Children whose parents use induction are more likely to make prosocial responses to the distress of others and to be more helpful than children whose parents do not use induction.

10. Aggression tends to be less hostile and more instrumental as children grow older.

FILL-IN-THE-BLANKS: Read the following sentences and write the missing word or words in the space provided.

1. The term _____ refers to an individual's assessment of his or her attributes and traits, and the term _____ refers to the negative and positive values that individuals assign to their attributes.

2. Psychologists who have studied what they call _____ have found that three-year-old children classified as _____ show strong tendencies toward conformity, inhibition and undue delay of gratification. In sharp contrast, children who are classified as _____ tend to be emotionally expressive and spontaneous but distractible and unable to delay gratification.

3. Studies have revealed that children who were _____ at age three were shy and inhibited at age seven. The combination of _____ and _____ at age three was predictive of excellent adjustment at age seven, whereas the combination of _____ and _____ predicted poor adjustment at age seven.

4. The term _____ describes the ways in which biological gender and its cultural association are incorporated into the child's self-perceptions and behavior.

5. The four features of sex typing are _____, which refers to the fundamental sense of being either a girl or boy; _____ ,which refers to the sense of being masculine or feminine; _____, which involves acting in ways that are culturally defined as feminine or masculine; and _____, which refers to what a person values or would like to be.

6. Most children have a sense of _____, or the understanding that gender does not change over time, by the age of _____ or _____.

7. Kohlberg proposed that sex typing results from _____ changes; Mischel's social learning theory approach proposed that sex typing is learned through _____ and _____; and _____ theory argues that children's cognitions about gender explain sex typing.

8. Studies indicate that _____ children are aware of ethnic differences earlier than _____ children.

9. The contradiction between self-esteem and group attitudes revealed in current research may reflect the difference between _____ identity and _____ identity.

10. Studies reveal that _____ modeling results in increased helping, verbalizations, and actions only in imaginary situations.

ANSWERS TO PRACTICE TEST ITEMS

MIX-AND-MATCH

1.	e	2.	h
3.	j	4.	l
5.	a	6.	d
7.	c	8.	k
9.	b	10.	n
11.	i	12.	g
13.	f	14.	m

MULTIPLE CHOICE

1.	b	2.	b
3.	a	4.	c
5.	a	6.	b
7.	d	8.	d
9.	c	10.	d

TRUE AND FALSE

1.	true	2.	true
3.	true	4.	true
5.	true	6.	true
7.	false	8.	false
9.	true	10.	false

FILL-IN-THE-BLANKS

1. self-concept; self-esteem
2. ego control; overcontrollers; undercontrollers
3. overcontrollers; high ego control; high ego resilience; high ego control; low ego resilience
4. sex typing
5. gender identity; sex role identity; sex role adoption; sex role preference
6. gender constancy; five; six
7. cognitive-developmental; instrumental conditioning; observation; schema
8. minority; nonminority
9. group; personal
10. symbolic

CHAPTER 12:
SOCIALIZATION IN THE FAMILY SETTING

CHAPTER OVERVIEW

Socialization is the process in which children acquire their social behavior, values and beliefs. Parents play an important role in the socialization of their children. For example, parents who are sensitive to a child's needs are more likely to promote emotional security and independence than parents who are less sensitive. Parents who believe that children are active learners are more likely to promote thinking and reasoning skills in their children than parents who believe children are passive learners. A child's personality and behavior also can affect the disciplinary practices of parents. Irritable or active children may elicit more negative evaluations and harsher discipline than children with milder temperaments.

The social context in which children are raised also plays an important role in their socialization. Parents who have secure marital relationships are more likely to use sensitive parenting, resulting in more secure parent-child relationships. Spousal support improves parenting practices by reducing emotional distress, modeling effective intervention strategies and by providing intervention when one partner is tired or the child is being extremely difficult. Studies also reveal that social support systems can reduce emotional stress and improve the quality of parenting.

Reward, punishment, induction, and imitation are frequently used to facilitate the development of self-regulation in children. Rewarding children can facilitate positive social behavior. The most appropriate rewards are those that immediately follow the behavior and are just sufficient to change the child's behavior in the desired direction. The use of punishment is most effective when it immediately follows the undesirable behavior, when it is administered by a loving and nurturant parent, when it is consistent, and when it is just sufficient to change the behavior. Inductive techniques use reasoning as a way to positively change a child's behavior and have been shown to enhance children's moral maturity, reasoning and behavior. Finally, imitation and identification also can facilitate children's social behavior. Studies indicate that children more readily identify with parents who are warm and nurturant.

Baumrind has identified four basic parenting styles that differentially effect socialization. Authoritative parents tend to have children who are socially competent, responsible, intelligent, and achievement-oriented. Daughters of authoritarian parents tend to be socially assertive, whereas daughters of rejecting-neglecting parents tend to lack social competence. Sons of rejecting-neglecting parents tend to be domineering but lacking in social competence and leadership skills. Although discipline styles can significantly affect a child's socialization, it is possible that a child's temperament also may affect a parent's discipline style.

Variations in family structures also can affect socialization. Siblings can provide emotional support and facilitate positive traits such as cooperation and social sensitivity. Children reared in mother-only households tend to do less well in school and on measures of intelligence. Divorce may have an adverse affect on children, resulting in more cognitive, emotional and social problems in boys than in girls. Despite popular belief, children often benefit from having a stepparent, although stepfathers produce more benefits for boys than for girls.

It is estimated that over one million children are abused every year. Anger, frustration, social and economic stress, and the negative effects of abuse on the child's personality and behavior may increase the potential for abuse. Abused children are more likely to be aggressive, distrustful, and less empathic than children who are not abused. A systems approach to abuse analyzes family interactions and maintains that dyadic relationships affect the entire family. Its focus is to understand the way in which family structures affect and maintain abusive relationships.

CHAPTER OUTLINE: Use the outline provided below by writing information related to each topic in the margins of the outline, e.g., definitions of terms and elaboration of concepts.

I. Determinants of Child-Rearing Practices

   A. *Parental characteristics and beliefs*

   B. *Children's personality and behavior*

   C. *Social contexts*

II. Child-Rearing Practices and Their Consequences

   A. *Reinforcement*

   B. *Punishment*

   C. *Inductive techniques*

   D. *Imitation and identification*

   E. *Patterns and styles of parental behavior*

   F. *Toward a theory of disciplinary techniques*

III. Variations in Family Structure

   A. *Siblings*

   B. *What adults are in the home?*

   C. *Stepparents*

   D. *Unmarried parents*

IV. Family Problems and Child Abuse

   A. *Patterns of abuse*

   B. *Affects of abuse on children*

V. A Systems Approach to Family Socialization

   A. *What is the systems approach?*

   B. *Focus and goals of the systems approach*

KEY DEFINITIONS AND TERMS: Define the following concepts and terms Try to provide an example for each word or term you have defined to help clarify its meaning.

Socialization:

Reinforcers:

Punishment:

Time-out:

Minimum sufficiency principle:

Extinction:

Inductive techniques:

Imitation:

Identification:

Authoritarian parenting:

Authoritative parenting:

Systems approach:

REVIEW QUESTIONS: Below are questions that relate to key concepts and information covered in your textbook. Answer the questions as thoroughly and completely as possible. Try to provide examples to support your answer and to clarify meaning.

1. What are the goals of socialization and how do they vary from one culture to the next?

2. How can culture and a child's developmental level affect socialization and parenting practices? What are the three factors that influence parents' child-rearing practices that were identified by Belsky?

3. Discuss the way in which parental traits and characteristics, cognitions and beliefs about children's motivations and abilities and social orientations can affect parenting styles, disciplinary practices and a child's social-developmental outcome.

4. Discuss the way in which children's personality and behavior can affect parenting styles. Provide examples to support your answer.

5. Discuss the way in which marital relationships and social support systems can affect parenting styles.

6. Discuss the way in which reward can facilitate socialization in children. When and how should rewards be allocated by parents? Is it possible to over-reward a child? How can extinction be used to modify behavior?

7. Discuss the way in which punishment can modify behavior in children. What principles should parents follow when using punishment to change their children's behavior?

8. Describe the way in which induction techniques can be used to socialize children and modify their behavior. What are some of the positive effects that induction techniques can have on children's social development?

9. Discuss the way in which children acquire their parents' behavior patterns, idiosyncrasies, motives, attitudes, and values through imitation and identification.

10. Describe the four styles of parental discipline identified by Baumrind. According to the results of her longitudinal study, how do the various discipline styles affect the socialization of children?

11. Describe Grusec and Goodnow's theory of parental discipline. What are the two steps in children's processing of parental discipline identified in their model?

12. Discuss the way in which siblings can affect each other's socialization and the long-term effects of sibling relationships. Are only children more likely to develop socialization problems than children with siblings?

13. Discuss the effect that father absence can have on the social development of children. What are some of the traits of children raised in mother-only households?

14. Discuss the way in which divorce can affect parent-child relationships. Do relationships appear to improve or worsen with time? What are some of the negative effects that divorce can have on children? Does divorce affect boys and girls differently? Are the negative effects of divorce usually permanent or do they dissipate over time?

15. Discuss the effects that stepparents have on children. Overall, do stepparents have a positive or negative effect on their stepchildren? How do boys and girls differ in their relationship with their stepparents?

16. Discuss the research that has examined the effect that unmarried parents can have on their children's social development. What effects can age have on the unmarried mother and her offspring? What do longitudinal studies reveal about the long-term consequences for adolescent mothers?

17. Approximately how many children are abused by their parents each year? What are some of the factors that are associated with child abuse? What are some of the effects that parental abuse can have on a child's personal and social development? What are some of the ways that child abuse can be effectively treated?

18. Describe the systems approach to family socialization. According to this view, how do family dynamics and interaction affect each member of the family?

MIX-AND-MATCH: In the left-hand column below are some key concepts or definitions. Choose the term from the column on the right that best matches each definition provided in the column on the left.

1. The process through which children acquire the behavior, skills, motives, values, beliefs, and standards that are characteristic, appropriate and desirable in their culture

    a. Authoritative parenting

2. Social or nonsocial rewards that can be used to modify children's behavior

    b. Identification

3. The principle that states the most effective way of changing a child's behavior over the long term is to provide rewards that are just sufficient to engage the child in the new behavior

    c. Grusec and Goodnow

4. Withdrawing reward or ignoring behavior in order to eliminate undesirable behavior

    d. Authoritarian parenting

5. A behavioral principle in which a prohibited activity is prevented by having the child sit on the sidelines for a short time without any attention from adults or other children

    e. Imitation

6. Technique that uses reasoning about misdeeds to socialize and discipline children

    f. Minimum-sufficiency

7. A process whereby individuals incorporate the characteristics and global behavior patterns of another person

    g. Reinforcers

8. Parenting style identified by Baumrind that is most likely to facilitate positive outcomes, such as social competence, intelligence and responsibility

    h. Time out

9. Parenting style identified by Baumrind that is most likely to facilitate negative outcomes, such as social incompetence and deficiencies in leadership

    i. Socialization

10. Researchers whose model of parental discipline focuses on the way that children process, understand and accept a disciplinary message

    j. Extinction

11. The model that stresses family relationships and dynamics and the effect that family patterns can have on child abuse

    k. Systems approach

12. The act of copying another person's behavior

    m. Induction

MULTIPLE CHOICE QUESTIONS: Read the following questions and indicate your answer by marking the option that you think best answers each question.

1. Which of the following was not cited by Belsky as a factor that influences parents' child-rearing practices?
   a. the gender of the child
   b. forces emanating from within the parent
   c. attributes of the child
   d. the social context in which the parent-child relationship is embedded

2. Parents who are nurturing and sensitive to their child's needs tend to have children who
   a. are emotionally and psychologically dependent.
   b. are low in achievement motivation.
   c. are emotional secure and independent.
   d. exhibit both "a" and "b."

3. In order for punishment to be effective, it should
   a. be severe so that its effects will be long lasting.
   b. be delayed so that the child has sufficient time to think about the misbehavior.
   c. be just severe enough to induce compliance.
   d. incorporate both "a" and "b,"

4. Parents who use inductive discipline techniques tend to have children who
   a. are hostile and aggressive as adults.
   b. are emotionally and psychologically dependent.
   c. are shy and inhibited.
   d. develop moral maturity, reasoning and behavior.

5. Research by Baumrind revealed that daughters of authoritarian parents tended to be
   a. socially assertive.
   b. shy and withdrawn.
   c. hostile and aggressive.
   d. lacking in social competence.

6. Research by Baumrind revealed that daughters of permissive and rejecting-neglecting parents tended to be
   a. socially assertive.
   b. shy and withdrawn.
   c. hostile and aggressive.
   d. lacking in social competence.

7. Studies reveal that older siblings tend to be
   a. lower in achievement motivation than younger siblings.
   b. higher in achievement motivation than younger siblings.
   c. dominant and initiate more social interactions.
   d. intellectually superior to younger siblings as adults.

8. Research investigating the effect that stepparents have on children's social development has found that
   a. boys tend to benefit from having a stepparent, particularly stepfathers.
   b. girls with stepfathers tend to express more anxiety than girls in intact families.
   c. the majority of boys and girls have negative attitudes toward stepparents of either sex.
   d. both "a" and "b" are true.

9. The effect that family relationships and family dynamics can have on the development and maintenance of abusive relationships is a central focus of
   a. social learning theory.
   b. the Grusec and Goodnow model.
   c. the systems approach.
   d. Kohlberg's cognitive-developmental theory.

10. Research that has studied the long-term effects of child abuse has revealed that
    a. abused children often grow up to be abusive parents.
    b. abusive mothers tend to be less intelligent than mothers who do not abuse their children.
    c. the incidence of child abuse increases as unemployment rates increase.
    d. all of the above are true.

TRUE AND FALSE QUESTIONS: Read the following statements and indicate whether you think each statement is true or false.

1. The quality of marital relationships is unrelated to parental styles.

2. Children who are severely or harshly punished by their parents are more likely to internalize rules of discipline than children who are punished less harshly.

3. Induction techniques of discipline enhance children's ability to feel guilt and shame.

4. Children are more likely to identify with parents who are warm and nurturing than with parents who are cold and rejecting.

5. Daughters of authoritarian parents tend to be deficient in leadership skills and lacking in social competence.

6. Older siblings tend to be dominant, initiate more interactions, and give more orders and suggestions.

7. The majority of children report extremely negative attitudes toward their stepparents.

8. Children reared in mother-only households perform less well in school and on tests of intelligence and achievement than children raised in two-parent households.

9. Parents tend to be less affectionate and more restrictive with their children the first few months following a divorce.

10. According to systems theory, a dyadic relationship in a family has little or no impact on other relationships within the family.

FILL-IN-THE-BLANKS: Read the following sentences and write the missing word or words in the space provided.

1. According to Belsky, parents' child-rearing practices can be influenced by forces emanating from within the _____, from attributes of the _____ and from the broader _____ in which the parent-child relationship is embedded.

2. Better marital relationships are associated with more _____ parenting, even when the effects of parents' individual psychological health are controlled.

3. Social support networks seem to play a particularly significant role under conditions of _____. Social support appears to have its primary effect on parenting by influencing parents' _____.

4. Rewards for positive social behavior tend to be the most effective when they are given _____ after the desired behavior has occurred and when the rewards are just _____ to engage the child in the new behavior.

5. Punishment from a _____, _____ parent is more likely to produce the desired result than punishment from a _____ or _____ parent.

6. The principle of discipline in which children sit on the sidelines for a short time without any attention from adults or other children is known as _____.

7. Daughters of _____ parents tend to be socially assertive whereas daughters of _____ or _____ parents tend to lack social competence.

8. According to the Grusec and Goodnow model of parental discipline, children must first _____ and then _____ the disciplinary message.

9. According to Grusec and Goodnow's model, two important factors that influence children's acceptance of discipline are whether the discipline is perceived as _____ to the misdeed and whether the child is _____ to accept the message.

10. Research on sibling relationships has revealed that first-born males tend to use more techniques based on _____ with their younger siblings, whereas first-born females are more likely to _____, _____, and _____ with their younger brothers and sisters.

MIX-AND-MATCH

1. i	2. g
3. f	4. j
5. h	6. m
7. b	8. d
9. d	10. c
11. k	12. e

MULTIPLE CHOICE

1. a	2. c
3. c	4. d
5. a	6. d
7. c	8. d
9. c	10. d

TRUE AND FALSE

1. false	2. false
3. true	4. true
5. false	6. true
7. false	8. true
9. true	10. false

FILL-IN-THE-BLANKS

1. parents; child; social context
2. sensitive
3. stress; emotionality
4. immediately; sufficient
5. nurturant; affectionate; cold; hostile
6. time out
7. authoritarian; permissive; rejecting-neglecting
8. understand; accept
9. appropriate; motivated
10. physical power; explain; ask; take turns

CHAPTER 13:
SOCIALIZATION BEYOND THE FAMILY

CHAPTER OVERVIEW

Peers play an important role in the socialization process. Research indicates that social interactions and play activity facilitate cooperation in children and a better understanding of rules. Children's perception of others becomes more abstract and complex as they grow older, and they are more likely to consider situational and cognitive factors in the evaluation of their peers. Changes in peer relations may be partially due to the development of empathy and role taking skills, which give children the ability to understand another person's perspective.

Popular children tend to be high in social and cognitive skills, whereas rejected children tend to be low in social and cognitive skills and are often aggressive. Neglected children are low in aggression and sociability, while controversial children are high in aggression but are also high in social and cognitive skills. Studies reveal that popular children tend to have mothers who are positive and sensitive in their interactions with them, while mothers of unpopular children tend to be negative and controlling. Studies also indicate that children's level of popularity remains fairly stable throughout the school years and may be a reliable indicator of future behavior.

Friendships also change as children become older. Whereas friendships among preschool children tend to be instrumental and short lived, friendships among older children tend to be longer-lasting and more personal and intimate. The development of friendships is related to communication clarity, information exchange, establishing common ground, resolution of conflict, positive reciprocity, and self-disclosure. Younger children tend to maintain friendships with those who live nearby and share similar interests, while older children are more likely to maintain friendships with those who have similar interests, attitudes and social orientations.

Some studies indicate that day care promotes the development of positive social skills in children, while other studies report opposite findings. The contradictory findings may be partially due to the quality of day care. Children in high-quality facilities tend to have better verbal and social skills, whereas children in low-quality facilities tend to be less self-regulatory and task-oriented. Research also reveals that highly structured classrooms tend to promote learning and cooperation, while less structured classrooms promote more peer interactions and imaginative play. In elementary school, teachers' expectations may affect socialization by causing them to unintentionally promote the behavior in children that they are expecting. Encouraging cooperation among students improves learning and facilitates peer relations, although mainstreaming has a weak effect on children's relations with handicapped students.

Research reveals that children watch between two and three hours of television per day. However, the amount of viewing time for elementary school children is not significantly related to whether or not the mother is employed. Television reduces children's participation in sports, clubs, dances, and social activities, but does not affect the amount of time spent reading. Television also has been linked to obesity, low levels of achievement and the development and reduction of negative stereotypes. Although violent television may increase aggressive behavior in children, television with prosocial content has been shown to promote altruism and sympathy.

Approximately twenty-one percent of the children in the United States live below the poverty level. Of the estimated two million homeless in the United States, the vast majority are families with children who must live in cramped and unsanitary conditions. Studies reveal that poverty adversely affects children's cognitive and social development. Loss of income, such as unemployment, also increases behavioral problems in children. The effects are similar for children of divorced women ,who most often experience a significant reduction in their income.

CHAPTER OUTLINE: Use the outline provided below by writing information related to each topic in the margins of the outline, e.g., definitions of terms and elaboration of concepts.

I.   **Relationships with Peers**

    A.   *Developmental changes in peer interactions*

    B.   *Peer relations and group structure*

    C.   *Concepts of friendship*

    D.   *Friendship formation*

    E.   *Maintenance of friendships*

II. **Day Care and School as Contexts for Development**

    A.   *Effects of early group care*

    B.   *Adult structuring*

    C.   *Elementary school*

    D.   *Teachers' expectations*

    E.   *Cooperative learning vs. competition*

    F.   *Desegregation and integration*

    G.   *Mainstreaming*

III. **Television as a Socializing Influence**

    A.   *Description of children's television viewing*

    B.   *Parents' influence on children's viewing*

    C.   *Effects of television on children's development*

    D.   *How children understand television*

    F.   *What is learned from television*

IV. **Government and Economic Influences**

    A.   *Social trends and social policy*

    B.   *Relations between the family and other social systems*

KEY DEFINITIONS AND TERMS: Define the following concepts and terms Try to provide an example for each word or term you have defined to help clarify its meaning.

Sociometric techniques:

Role taking:

Empathy:

Popular children:

Neglected children:

Rejected children:

Controversial children:

High-quality day care:

Low-quality day care:

Adult structuring:

Teacher expectancies:

Cooperative learning:

Mainstreaming:

REVIEW QUESTIONS: Below are questions that relate to key concepts and information covered in your textbook. Answer the questions as thoroughly and completely as possible. Try to provide examples to support your answer and to clarify meaning.

1. Describe some of the changes in peer relations that occur as children become older. What are some of the benefits of play? How does the development of empathy and role-taking skills change peer relations? With what behaviors and traits is role-taking ability correlated? How do children's conceptions of others change as they grow older and why?

2. Describe the behaviors and traits of the following types of children: popular children, rejected children, neglected children, and controversial children. Discuss the way in which peer interactions may be acquired and generalized from children's relationships within their families.

3. In what way do peer relations in children predict later outcome? Why do some children have difficulties in their social relationships? Describe some of the ways in which children can be trained to improve their social skills.

4. How do concepts of friendships change as children grow older? What are the six social processes related to friendship formation? In what way can a parent's style of interacting with his or her child serve as a model for a child's approach to friendship development?

5. Discuss the way in which the maintenance of friendships changes as children grow older. How do friends foster each other's cognitive and emotional growth?

6. What are some of the contradictory findings that studies have revealed about the effect of day care on children's socialization? Discuss the various ways in which the overall quality of day care can affect children's development. How do low-quality and high-quality day care facilities differ?

7. Discuss the effect that adult structuring can have on the social and cognitive development in children. What traits in children are associated with highly structured classrooms? What traits are associated with less structured classrooms? In what way does gender affect the type of structure children prefer?

8. Describe the research that has investigated the effect that teachers' expectations can have on children's academic performance. How are teacher expectancies communicated to children?

9.   Describe a method used to promote cooperative learning in the classroom. What are the positive effects that cooperative learning can have on children's cognitive and social development?

10.   What is meant by "social" segregation? What are some of the ways that interracial and cross-ethnic friendships can be promoted by school organizations?

11. Discuss the research that has examined the effects of "mainstreaming" handicapped children into traditional classroom settings. How successful have efforts been to promote relations between handicapped and nonhandicapped children?

12. How many hours do American children spend watching television? What did the longitudinal study from the university of Kansas reveal about the type of television programming children watch? How do children of employed mothers differ from the children of unemployed mothers in the amount of time they spend watching television? How can parents make the television programs children watch more profitable?

13. In what way does television viewing affect children's participation in other activities, such as sports, clubs, dances and the amount of time spent reading? What have studies revealed about the relationships between television viewing and health and fitness, school achievement and cognitive processes and intellectual passivity?

14. How do children understand television? What features of television programs are most likely to capture children's attention? Discuss the way in which children's cognitive development affects their understanding of television programs.

15. What do children learn from television? Discuss the role that television can play in the development as well as the reduction of negative stereotypes. How does television affect aggression and prosocial behavior in children?

16. How many children in the United States live at or below the poverty level? What factors account for the increasing number of children living in poverty? What are some of the effects that poverty can have on children's development?

17. How can a reduction of income, such as unemployment, affect the socialization and development of children? Does a mother's unemployment have the same affect as a father's unemployment? How do governmental policies affect mother-headed households? Discuss homelessness in America. Are the majority of homeless single individuals or families with children?

18. Discuss the way in which relations between the family differs in other social systems.

MIX-AND-MATCH: In the left-hand column below are some key concepts or definitions. Choose the term from the column on the right that best matches each definition provided in the column on the left.

1. Research method used to study peer relations in which children are asked to list the names of children whom they like and do not like

   a. Popular children

2. The ability to put oneself mentally in someone else's position, which is believed to influence children's perception of others as they become older

   b. High-quality day care

3. The term that refers to the recognition, understanding and vicarious feeling of another person's emotions

   c. Neglected children

4. Children who are high in social and cognitive skills and who tend to be well liked by their peers

   d. Cooperative learning

5. Children who tend to be high in aggression and low in sociability and cognitive skills, and who often act in immature, antisocial, disruptive, and deviant ways

   e. Low-quality day care

6. Children who tend to be low in both aggression and in sociability and are often shy and withdrawn

   f. Role -aking

7. Children who are high in aggression, but are also high in social and cognitive skills, resulting in equal mixtures of like and dislike from other children

   g. Mainstreaming

8. Day care facilities that tend to have higher adult-child ratios, frequent adult-child interaction, smaller group sizes and are more likely to facilitate the development of verbal and cognitive skills

   h. Adult structuring

9. Day care facilities that tend to have larger group sizes, less equipment, fewer adult-child interactions, and less likely to facilitate verbal and cognitive skills

   i. Sociometric techniques

10. The input that teachers have on the types of activities and tasks in which children engage and the amount of control the teacher has in directing their activities

    k. Controversial children

11. Type of learning situation in which children study and learn together in small, interdependent groups, which improves learning and promotes positive self-esteem and attitudes toward other students

    l. Empathy

12. Term used that refers to the integration of handicapped students into traditional classrooms

    m. Rejected children

MULTIPLE CHOICE QUESTIONS: Read the following questions and indicate your answer by marking the option that you think best answers each question.

1. Children who are high in aggression and low in social and cognitive skills are called
   a. rejected children.
   b. neglected children.
   c. controversial children.
   d. competitive children.

2. Children who are high in aggression and also high in cognitive and social skills are called
   a. rejected children.
   b. neglected children.
   c. controversial children.
   d. competitive children.

3. Research that has compared the amount of time children of employed vs. unemployed mothers spend watching television has revealed that
   a. children of employed mothers watch more television during the preschool years.
   b. children of unemployed mothers watch more television during the preschool years.
   c. there are no differences in viewing time by the time children go to elementary school.
   d. both "b" and "c" are true.

4. Research on children's personality, behavior and popularity has revealed that
   a. interactions with peers is not related to children's relationships within their families.
   b. providing children with "social skills" training does not affect their peer relations.
   c. children's relationships with peers seem to be sensitive indicators of later outcome.
   d. children's relationships with peers do not reliably predict later outcome.

5. As children grow older, their friendships tend to be
   a. based more on cooperation, trust and reciprocity.
   b. based more on convenience than on similarities.
   c. shorter-lived and less enduring.
   d. based more on superficial qualities, such as "status," than on genuine affection.

6. Which of the following is not one of the six social processes related to friendship formation cited in your textbook?
   a. information exchange
   b. social and economic status
   c. positive reciprocity
   d. self-disclosure

7. Research on the effects of early group care has revealed that
   a. early group care has a negative effect on children's social and cognitive development.
   b. early group care has a positive effect on children's social and cognitive development.
   c. early group care has no effect on children's social and cognitive development.
   d. the effects of early group care are related to the overall quality of the day care facility.

8. Research has revealed that approximately _____ percent of the children living in the United States are living at or below the level of poverty.
   a. 10
   b. 21
   c. 37
   d. 55

9. Which of the following is not associated with high-quality day care?
   a. small group sizes
   b. low adult-child ratios
   c. frequent adult-child interactions
   d. amount of equipment available to children

10. Research reveals that encouraging cooperative learning in school
   a. improves learning.
   b. contributes to positive attitudes toward other students.
   c. improves children's self-esteem.
   d. promotes all of the above.

TRUE AND FALSE QUESTIONS: Read the following statements and indicate whether you think each statement is true or false.

1. The preschool children of employed mothers watch more hours of television than the preschool children of mothers who stay at home.

2. The percentage of children in the United States who are living at or below the poverty has significantly declined since the 1960s.

3. Providing social skills training to isolated and rejected children can significantly improve social relationships with their peers.

4. As children grow older, their friendships become more stable and enduring.

5. Research reveals that early group care has a negative effect on children's social and cognitive development, regardless of the day care facility.

6. Studies on mainstreaming reveal that nonhandicapped children interact more with other nonhandicapped peers than with handicapped children.

7. Watching television reduces children's participation in community activities, such as sports, clubs, dances, and parties.

8. Watching television significantly reduces the amount of time children spend reading.

9. Viewing violent television increases aggressive behavior in children.

10. Fathers who experience economic stress tend to become more punitive and their children are more prone to tantrums and angry outbursts.

FILL-IN-THE-BLANKS: Read the following sentences and write the missing word or words in the space provided.

1. Children who are high in cognitive and social skills are called _____ children; _____ children are high in aggression and low in social and cognitive skills; _____ children are low in aggression and sociability; _____ children are high in aggression and are also high in cognitive and social skills.

2. The six social processes related to friendship formation include connectedness and _____ clarity; _____ exchange; establishing _____; resolution of _____; positive _____; and _____.

3. High-quality day care tends to have _____ adult-child ratios and _____ group sizes. When groups are small, children tend to engage in more _____ and _____ play.

4. Cooperative learning facilitates _____, improves children's _____ and also promotes better _____ with peers.

5. Friendly relations among members of different ethnic groups are more likely when the school organization promotes _____ rather than _____ and when individual achievement is _____.

6. Research findings reveal that children watch an estimated _____ to _____ hours of television per day. Watching television has been shown to _____ children's participation in activities such as sports, clubs, dances, and parties.

7. Studies show a small relationship between the amount of time viewing television and _____ levels of achievement. The negative effects of television on reading are relatively _____.

8. Television programs with violent content have been shown to significantly increase _____ in children. Television programs with positive messages have been shown to increase _____ behavior in children.

9. Approximately _____ percent of the children in the United States live at or below the poverty level, a rate that has _____ since the 1960s and is at least _____ that of other industrialized nations.

10. In the United States, children are considered to be the sole responsibility of their _____. In others cultures, the responsibility for socializing children is shared by _____, _____, and institutions that are outside of the _____.

MIX-AND-MATCH

1.	i	2.	f
3.	l	4.	a
5.	m	6.	c
7.	k	8.	b
9.	e	10.	h
11.	d	12.	g

MULTIPLE CHOICE

1.	a	2.	c
3.	d	4.	c
5.	a	6.	b
7.	d	8.	b
9.	b	10.	d

TRUE AND FALSE

1.	false	2.	false
3.	true	4.	true
5.	false	6.	true
7.	true	8.	false
9.	true	10.	true

FILL-IN-THE-BLANKS

1. popular; rejected; neglected; controversial
2. communication; information; common ground; conflict; reciprocity; self-disclosure
3. higher; smaller; fantasy; imaginative
4. learning; self-esteem; relations
5. cooperation; competition; deemphasized
6. two; three; reduce
7. lower; small
8. aggression; prosocial
9. twenty-one; increased; double
10. parents; individuals; communities; family

CHAPTER 14:
ADOLESCENCE

CHAPTER OVERVIEW

Adolescence begins with the onset of puberty, when the pituitary gland signals the body to increase its production of sex hormones. Increases in testosterone facilitate the development of primary and secondary sex characteristics in boys and increases in estrogen and progesterone facilitate the development of primary and secondary sex characteristics in girls. Adolescence is also characterized by a growth spurt, which peaks at age 13 for males and at age 11 for females. As a general rule, females begin and end their growth spurt about two years earlier than boys.

The first visible sign of puberty in males is an increase in the size of the testes and scrotum, followed by an increase in height and penis size about a year later. Axillary and facial hair appear about two years following the appearance of pubic hair. The first visible sign of puberty in females is pubic hair, followed by the beginning of breast development, axillary hair and increases in estrogen. Within a year the uterus, vagina, labia and clitoris begin to develop. The onset of menstruation occurs relatively late in puberty, at the approximate age of 12.75 years. It is important to recognize that variations in the timing of development during puberty are normal.

In addition to physical changes, numerous psychological changes also occur during puberty. Some females view menstruation as a symbol of maturity and have better self-esteem following menarche, while others acquire negative attitudes that may worsen their experience with menstruation. Although males are often proud of their emerging sexuality, they may also become self-conscious and concerned about spontaneous erections and ejaculations. Timing of puberty can also have psychological effects on adolescents. For example, boys who develop early are often more athletic and self-confident but tend to avoid problem solving and new situations. Late-maturing boys are often less athletic but tend to be more intellectually curious and more likely to engage in exploratory behavior. Conversely, early-maturing girls tend to be larger, heavier, moodier, and less confident than later maturing girls, although the effects of early puberty tend to be worse for girls with personality and behavioral problems prior to puberty.

Adolescence is also a time when sexual feelings and behavior begin to change. Over half of the females in the United States have had intercourse by the age of 18, and over half of the males have had intercourse by the age of 17. Although the proportion of sexually active males and females increases with age, males are more likely than females to have had sexual intercourse across all age groups, a finding that may be due to higher levels of testosterone and more relaxed sexual standards for males. Sexually active teenagers are at risk for pregnancy and for contracting sexually transmitted diseases. Teenage girls who become pregnant are significantly more likely to drop out of school and end up on welfare than girls who wait until their 20s to have a baby. Despite the belief that providing information about sex may increase sexual promiscuity, studies reveal that teenagers who feel comfortable talking about sex with their parents are actually less likely to engage in premarital sex. Adolescence also may be a time when teenagers may need to address issues related to their sexual orientation. It is important for teenagers to resolve sexual orientation conflicts in order for their adolescent identity to fully develop.

Important cognitive changes also occur during adolescence. According to Piaget, adolescence is a time when individuals become capable of formal operations, which include the ability to reason about hypothetical problems and to systematically search for solutions. Although Piaget proposed that these skills emerge during adolescence, newer research reveals that the age of onset is more variable and that the change is less sudden and less universal than he originally claimed. However, in line with Piaget, adolescents become more efficient in their information-processing skills and capable of processing more complex information as they grow older.

CHAPTER OUTLINE: Use the outline provided below by writing information related to each topic in the margins of the outline, e.g., definitions of terms and elaboration of concepts.

I. **Physical Growth in Adolescence**

   A. *Hormonal factors in development*

   B. *The adolescent growth spurt*

   C. *Sexual development in males*

   D. *Sexual development in females*

   E. *Normal variations in development*

II. **Psychological Aspects of Maturation**

   A. *Onset of puberty in females*

   B. *Onset of puberty in males*

   C. *Early and late maturation in males*

   D. *Early and late maturation in females*

III. **Adolescent Sexuality**

   A. *Premarital sexual intercourse*

   B. *Sexually transmitted diseases*

   C. *Pregnancy*

   D. *Contraception*

   E. *Homosexual behavior and orientation*

IV. **Cognitive Development in Adolescence**

   A. *Formal operations*

   B. *Critique of Piaget*

   C. *Information-processing skills*

KEY DEFINITIONS AND TERMS: Define the following concepts and terms Try to provide an example for each word or term you have defined to help clarify its meaning.

Adolescence:

Puberty:

Pituitary gland:

Testosterone:

Estrogens:

Progestins:

Growth spurt:

Menarche:

Early-maturing boys:

Late-maturing boys:

Early-maturing girls:

Late-maturing girls:

Contraception:

REVIEW QUESTIONS: Below are questions that relate to key concepts and information covered in your textbook. Answer the questions as thoroughly and completely as possible. Try to provide examples to support your answer and to clarify meaning.

1. When does adolescence begin and end? When does puberty begin and what are the mechanisms that trigger the beginning of puberty? What role do the hypothalamus, pituitary gland and sex hormones play in puberty?

2. Describe the adolescent growth spurt. When does it usually begin for males and females and how long does it usually last? Which parts of the body grow early and which parts tend to grow later in the growth spurt?

3. Describe the sexual development in males. What is the first outward sign of impending sexual maturity? When and in what order do the various sexual changes that accompany puberty in males occur?

4. Describe the sexual development in females. What is the first outward sign of impending sexual maturity? When and in what order do the various sexual changes that accompany puberty in females occur?

5. Describe some of the normal variations in sexual development during puberty. What are some of the factors that affect normal variations in puberty? What role, if any, may psychological factors play in the onset of menstruation?

6. Discuss some of the positive and negative psychological effects that maturation and puberty can have on males and females.

7. What are some of the positive and negative effects that early vs. late maturation can have on males?

8. What are some of the positive and negative effects that early vs. late maturation can have on females? Why is early maturation a more favorable event for boys and a negative one for girls?

9. Describe the research that has investigated premarital sexual intercourse in teenagers. By what age have the majority of males had sexual intercourse? By what age have the majority of females had sexual intercourse? Why are males more likely to have had intercourse across all age groups?

10. Discuss the research that has examined differences in sexual intercourse as a function of socioeconomic class and ethnic background. What has research revealed about class and ethnic differences in sexual patterns of behavior?

11. What are the chances that a sexually active teenager will become pregnant within a year? What percentage of teenagers now report using contraception the first time they have intercourse? How does the use of contraceptives the first time change with a woman's age? How well do teenagers use contraceptives?

12. In the United States, what percentage of teenage girls between aged 15 to 19 become pregnant every year? What percentage are unmarried? How do adolescent pregnancy rates in the United States compare to the rates in Great Britain, Canada, New Zealand, Finland, Denmark and the Netherlands?

13. What are the social, psychological, educational and economic disadvantages associated with adolescent pregnancy? How do sexually active adolescent girls who do not use contraceptives compare psychologically with those who use contraceptives regularly? What are some of the traits of males adolescents who are most likely to use contraceptive measures? What are some of the reasons adolescents avoid using contraceptives?

14. Do most teenage girls intentionally become pregnant? What are some of the reasons for which females have intentionally becoming pregnant?

15. Do studies support or refute the claim that providing information about sex increases promiscuity among teenagers? What are the characteristics of effective school-based pregnancy- and STD-prevention programs, summarized by Kirby?

16. According to a recent national survey, what percentage of males and females living in the United States are exclusively homosexual? Describe the four stages of sexual identity reorganization that adolescents often go through, according to Troiden.

17. Describe the stage of formal operations proposed by Piaget. What are the common features of this stage and what are some of the ways that Piaget tested cognitive abilities in this stage? What were some of problems found with Piaget's formulation of a stage of formal operations?

18. Describe some of the additional cognitive changes experienced during adolescence from an information-processing perspective. Compare the information-processing view to Piaget's formal operations.

MIX-AND-MATCH: In the left-hand column below are some key concepts or definitions. Choose the term from the column on the right that best matches each definition provided in the column on the left.

1. The developmental period that begins with the onset of puberty and ends with the assumption of adult responsibilities

2. The phase of adolescence during which individuals become physically and sexually mature

3. The structure located at the base of the brain that begins releasing previously inhibited hormones at the onset of puberty

4. The accelerated rate of increase in height and weight that occurs at puberty

5. The hormone that triggers the development of physical and sexual changes in males

6. Term that refers to the onset of menstruation

7. Males who tend to be athletic and self-confident but who may avoid problem-solving or new situations unless they are urged

8. Males who are likely to have a harder time excelling in sports and establishing relationships with females but who tend to be more intellectually curious and higher in exploratory behavior and social initiative

9. The feminizing hormones

10. Females who tend to be bigger, heavier, moodier, show more behavioral problems and precocious sexual behavior, and who tend to be unpopular with their same-sex peers

11. Term that refers to any method that prevents pregnancy, such as birth-control pills, IUDs, diaphragms, and condoms

12. The pregnancy hormones

a. Testosterone

b. Early-maturing males

c. Puberty

d. Late-maturing males

e. Early-maturing females

f. Contraception

g. Adolescence

h. Progestins

i. Pituitary gland

j. Growth spurt

k. Menarche

l. Estrogens

235

MULTIPLE CHOICE QUESTIONS: Read the following questions and indicate your answer by marking the option that you think best answers each question.

1. The adolescent growth spurt in females
   a. begins two years later than it does in males.
   b. ends about two years later than it does in males.
   c. begins and ends about two years earlier than it does in males.
   d. incorporates both "a" and "b."

2. The first outward sign of impending sexual maturity in males is
   a. an increase in the length and size of the penis.
   b. a deepening of the voice.
   c. an increase in the size of the testes and scrotum.
   d. the appearance of axillary and facial hair.

3. The first outward sign of impending sexual maturity in females is
   a. the appearance of unpigmented, downy pubic hair.
   b. the onset of menstruation.
   c. the enlargement of the labia and clitoris.
   d. the increase in the size of the uterus and vagina.

4. Research on premenarcheal expectations of menstruation has revealed that
   a. expectations are unrelated to a female's actual experience with menstruation.
   b. expectations are correlated with what females experience after menarche.
   c. postmenarcheal reports tend to be much more negative than premenarcheal expectations.
   d. discomfort during menstruation is caused totally by psychological factors.

5. Which of the following is <u>not</u> true about early maturing males?
   a. They tend to become involved in boy-girl relationships sooner.
   b. They tend to be more intellectually curious.
   c. They tend to have more self-confidence.
   d. They tend to have an advantage in many activities such as athletics.

6. Which of the following is <u>not</u> true about early maturing females?
   a. They tend to be more popular with their same-sex peers.
   b. They tend to be less satisfied with their body image than average or late maturers.
   c. They tend to be easily disorganized under stress.
   d. They tend to perform poorly in school and score lower on achievement tests.

7. Research on sexual intercourse as a function of socioeconomic class and ethnic background has revealed that
   a. black adolescents are more sexually active than whites or Hispanics.
   b. there are no significant differences between black adolescents and white adolescents.
   c. Hispanics are more sexually active than white and black adolescents.
   d. sexual activities among black adolescents have increased significantly in the last 20 years.

8. Recent research reveals that about _____ of American adolescents report using contraception the first time they have intercourse.
   a. ten percent
   b. one-quarter
   c. one-half
   d. two-thirds

9. Compared to other countries, such as Great Britain and the Netherlands, the pregnancy rate in the United States is
   a. significantly higher.
   b. significantly lower.
   c. about the same.
   d. higher than in Great Britain but lower than the Netherlands.

10. According to Piaget, which of the following is not a hallmark of the formal operations?
    a. the ability to engage in reversible operations
    b. the ability to reason about hypothetical problems
    c. the ability to think about possibilities as well as actualities
    d. the ability to systematically search for solutions

TRUE AND FALSE QUESTIONS: Read the following statements and indicate whether you think each statement is true or false.

1. In both males and females, the growth spurt lasts about six years.

2. The average age of menarche in the United States is 12.5 years.

3. There is very little variation in the timing and development that occur during puberty.

4. Research reveals that what premenarcheal girls expect of menstruation is correlated with what they report experiencing after menarche.

5. Late-maturing boys tend to be more intellectually curious and higher in exploratory behavior than early maturing boys.

6. Adolescents now do about as well as adult women at using contraceptive methods as they are designed to be used and in preventing unintended pregnancy.

7. In the United States about 11 percent of girls aged 15 to 19 become pregnant each year.

8. A recent survey revealed that the majority of teenage girls reported that they intentionally became pregnant.

9. Current studies reveal that the age of onset of formal operational thinking is less variable than Piaget envisaged.

10. Adolescents are able to process more, and more complex, information than younger children.

FILL-IN-THE-BLANKS: Read the following sentences and write the missing word or words in the space provided.

1. At the beginning of puberty, the cells of the _____ mature, and signals are sent to the _____ to begin releasing previously inhibited _____.

2. The masculinizing hormones are called the _____; the feminizing hormones are called the _____; and the pregnancy hormones are called the _____.

3. In both sexes, the adolescent growth spurt lasts about _____ years. For the average male, the growth rate peaks at age _____; in females this occurs at about age _____. In girls, the growth spurt usually begins and ends about _____ years earlier.

4. In males, the first outward sign of impending sexual maturity is an increase in the growth of the _____ and _____, which usually begins at about age _____. A definite lowering of the voice usually occurs fairly _____ in puberty.

5. In females, the first outward sign of impending sexual maturity is the appearance of unpigmented, downy _____, although the so-called bud stage of _____ development may sometimes precede it. The average age of first menstruation in the United States, called _____ , is about _____ years.

6. Compared to other countries, the adolescent pregnancy rate in the United States is significantly _____. Girls who have babies during adolescence are _____ as likely to drop out of school, less likely to gain _____; and more likely to end up on _____.

7. Studies reveal that females who do not use contraceptives or who use them rarely are more likely to have _____ attitudes; to feel _____ to control their lives; and to have a low sense of personal _____.

8. Among male adolescents, those who are most likely to employ contraceptive measures tend to be _____, more experienced in _____, and more organized and _____ in their general approach to life.

9. The common features of formal operational thought includes the ability to reason about _____ problems; to think about _____ as well as actualities; and to be able to _____ search for solutions to problems.

10. Research on information-processing reveals that adolescents are generally able to process more _____ information than younger children, and to do so more _____ and _____.

ANSWERS TO PRACTICE TEST ITEMS

MIX-AND-MATCH

1. g	2. c
3. i	4. j
5. a	6. k
7. e	8. d
9. l	10. e
11. f	12. h

MULTIPLE CHOICE

1. c	2. c
3. a	4. b
5. b	6. a
7. a	8. d
9. a	10. a

TRUE AND FALSE

1. false	2. true
3. false	4. true
5. true	6. true
7. true	8. false
9. false	10. true

FILL-IN-THE-BLANKS

1. hypothalamus; pituitary gland; hormones
2. testosterones; estrogens; progestins
3. 4.5; 13; 11; two
4. scrotum; testes; 12.5; late
5. pubic hair; breast; menarche; 12.75
6. higher; twice; employment; welfare
7. fatalistic; powerless; competence
8. older; dating; responsible
9. hypothetical; possibilities; systematically
10. complex; quickly; efficiently

239

CHAPTER 15:
AUTONOMY, INTIMACY, IDENTITY, AND VALUES IN ADOLESCENCE

CHAPTER OVERVIEW

Adolescents' relationships with their parents change in three important ways as they grow and mature. First, they begin to recognize that their parents have thoughts, feelings and roles outside of the family that make them unique individuals. Second, they tend to spend less time with their parents as they grow older. Third, they are more prone to conflict with their parents than when they were younger. Open and effective communication within the family facilitates identity formation and role-taking abilities in adolescents. Moreover, authoritative parents provide the warmth, supervision and psychological autonomy children need to make a successful transition into adolescence and also promote greater academic achievement in their children.

Peers play an important role in the psychological and social development of adolescents. Peer groups vary in their composition and membership, and the choice of peer groups depends largely on the characteristics of the adolescent. Conformity to peer pressure may be affected by an adolescent's socioeconomic background, relationship with parents and other adults, school environment, personality, age, and status with peers. Although peers exert a strong influence on adolescent development, parents influence their children's peer group values, the peer group to which their children choose to belong and their children's social and moral values.

Friendships are more intimate than peer relations and provide adolescents with the opportunity to explore their feelings. Friends often provide an important source of emotional support and adolescents increasingly value friends who are loyal, trustworthy and reliable as they grow older. Because friends provide adolescents with the opportunity to exchange ideas, experiences and feelings, they also play an important role in self-understanding and identity formation.

According to Erikson, the primary developmental task of adolescence is identity formation. An important phase of identify formation is the "moratorium," a period when adolescents actively question and explore who they are. Adolescents who do not question and explore who they are may experience "identity foreclosure." Some theorists propose that adolescents in identity foreclosure have a high need for approval that limits their development. Others argue that they merely have a respect for authority and more traditional values. Adolescents who never develop a sense of who they are go through a prolonged period of "identity diffusion" and tend to have low self-esteems, immature moral reasoning, and difficulties establishing relationships. Adolescents who develop a clear idea of who they are have developed "identity achievement" and tend to have a greater capacity for intimacy, a more confident sexual identity and a more positive self-esteem.

Psychologists also have studied changes in moral reasoning from childhood to adolescence. Piaget proposed that children's moral reasoning changes as their cognitive abilities become more abstract. For example, during the stage of moral realism, children believe that rules are handed down by authorities that are fixed and absolute. However, by age 10 or 11, children enter the stage of moral relativism and come to understand that rules can be changed by agreement or consensus. Kohlberg extended Piaget's theory by proposing that moral reasoning goes through six levels of development, progressing from rigid and conventional thinking to the consideration of abstract principles that may exceed the boundaries of conventional rules or laws. Although most adults reach levels three and four, the percentage of those who reach stage five or six is extremely small. Although studies confirm Kohlberg's hypotheses that stages of moral development are orderly, universal, and invariant, critics argue that morality is culturally relative and that his theory is ethnocentric. Gilligan argues that Kohlberg's methodology is gender biased and argues that moral reasoning differs for males and females. Finally, research reveals that moral reasoning is more likely to predict moral behavior for adults than for children.

CHAPTER OUTLINE: Use the outline provided below by writing information related to each topic in the margins of the outline, e.g., definitions of terms and elaboration of concepts.

I. **Parental Relationships and the Development of Autonomy**

   A. *Changing interaction patterns in the family*

   B. *Variations in parental behavior*

II. **Adolescents and their Peers**

   A. *Peer groups*

   B. *Friendships*

   C. *Romantic relationships*

   D. *Developing a sense of identity*

   E. *Varieties of identity status*

   F. *Entering the world of work*

III. **Moral Development and Values**

   A. *Piaget's approach*

   B. *Kohlberg's approach*

   C. *Research on Kohlberg's theory*

   D. *Criticisms of Kohlberg's theory*

   E. *Moral judgment and behavior*

KEY DEFINITIONS AND TERMS: Define the following concepts and terms Try to provide an example for each word or term you have defined to help clarify its meaning.

Peer groups:

Identity formation:

Moratorium:

Identity foreclosure:

Identity diffusion:

Identity achievement:

Moral development:

Moral reasoning:

Moral realism:

Moral relativism:

Preconventional morality:

Conventional morality:

Postconventional morality:

REVIEW QUESTIONS: Below are questions that relate to key concepts and information covered in your textbook. Answer the questions as thoroughly and completely as possible. Try to provide examples to support your answer and to clarify meaning.

1. Discuss the three ways in which adolescents' relationships with their parents change as they mature. Over what domains (e.g., moral issues, conventional behavior, personal behavior, etc.) are adolescents less likely to allow their parents to influence or control?

2. Discuss the ways that transitional difficulties and conflicts can be reduced between parents and adolescents. According to research, what is the variable that is associated with greater harmony and cohesiveness in families?

3. What type of parenting style is most likely to foster effective communication? What are the three components of authoritarian parenting during adolescence? What are the positive adolescent characteristics with which authoritarian parenting has been associated?

4. What are peer groups and what are some of the variations in peer group composition and structure that adolescents can easily identify? What are the functions that peer groups serve during an adolescent's social and psychological development?

5. Compare parental and peer influences and values during adolescent development. Are parental and peer values usually different or fundamentally similar and why? In what areas of adolescent development are parents more likely to have an influences than peers?

6. How does the nature of friendship change as children grow and mature? Discuss some of the fundamental differences between friendships and peer relations during adolescence. What role do friends play in adolescent development?

7. How did Erik Erikson and Harry Stack Sullivan differ in their views about romantic relationships in adolescence? Describe the observational study conducted by Dunphy in Australia. What transitions from same-sex friendships to romantic relationships were observed?

8. Discuss the way in which family influences affect adolescent identity formation. How do male and female identity formation differ with respect to family relationships and influences?

9. Describe the following types of identity status and the developmental outcomes associated with each: identity foreclosure, identity diffusion and identity achievement.

10. Describe research that has investigated the known effects of adolescent employment. What are some of the negative consequences with which employment is correlated? What are some of the explanations that have been offered?

11. Describe Piaget's theory of moral reasoning. What are the two stages of moral reasoning that were proposed by Piaget? According to Piaget, why does moral reasoning change as children become older?

12. What has subsequent research revealed about Piaget's theory? Are children capable of understanding another's intentions earlier or later than Piaget originally proposed?

13. Describe the research methodology used by Kohlberg to study moral reasoning How did the age of Kohlberg's subjects affect their response to Heinz's dilemma? What were the three levels and subdivisions of moral reasoning proposed by Kohlberg?

14. Describe the research that has supported Kohlberg's theory of moral reasoning. What aspects of his theory have been confirmed by subsequent research?

15. What are some of the criticisms that have been offered against Kohlberg's theory? What were some of the proposed methodological biases of his theory? According to Gilligan, how do males and females differ in their moral reasoning? What did her research reveal about the processes used by females in resolving a moral dilemma?

16. Describe research that has examined the relationship between moral judgment and moral behavior. Does moral judgment predict moral behavior? In what way does the relationship change with age?

MIX-AND-MATCH: In the left-hand column below are some key concepts or definitions. Choose the term from the column on the right that best matches each definition provided in the column on the left.

1. The ideal process of identity formation proposed by Erikson during which an adolescent proceeds through a period of questioning and exploration

2. An interruption in the process of identity formation in which an adolescent does not engage in a period of questioning and exploration

3. A prolonged period during which adolescents struggle with but are unable to develop a clear sense of their identity and which is associated with low self-esteem, impulsivity and disorganized thinking

4. Identity status of individuals who have a strong sense of who they are and who tend to be autonomous, creative, and complex in their thinking

5. Theorist who proposed that moral reasoning proceeds from the stage of moral realism to the stage of moral relativism

6. Theorist who proposed that moral reasoning may occur at the preconventional, conventional and postconventional level

7. Stage of moral development proposed by Piaget during which children perceive rules as rigid and fixed

8. Stage of moral reasoning proposed by Piaget during which children recognize that rules can be changed by agreement or consensus

9. Level of moral reasoning proposed by Kohlberg in which right and wrong are judged primarily by the consequences of actions

10. Level of moral reasoning proposed by Kohlberg in which the primary focus is on interpersonal relationships and social values that take precedence over individual interests

11. Level of moral development proposed by Kohlberg in which moral judgments are based on abstract principles that are believed to be inherently right rather than because society considers them right

12. The process whereby adolescents attempt to develop a sense of who they are, which Erikson believed was the central task of adolescence

a. Piaget

b. Postconventional level

c. Moral realism

d. Preconventional level

e. Moral relativism

f. Moratorium

g. Identity formation

h. Identity diffusion

i. Identity achievement

j. Identity foreclosure

k. Kohlberg

l. Conventional level

MULTIPLE CHOICE QUESTIONS: Read the following questions and indicate your answer by marking the option that you think best answers each question.

1. Which of the following is <u>not</u> one of the ways in which adolescents' relationships with their parents change?
   a. They are more prone to conflict with their parents.
   b. They are less prone to conflict with their parents.
   c. They are better able to differentiate parents as persons from the roles they play as parents.
   d. They spend less time with their parents.

2. Adolescents view their parents as exerting the <u>least</u> amount of influence regarding
   a. moral issues.
   b. conventional behavior.
   c. personal behavior.
   d. all of the above.

3. Which of the following is <u>not</u> a component of authoritative parenting in adolescence?
   a. warmth
   b. granting psychological autonomy
   c. behavioral supervision and monitoring
   d. greater control over an adolescent's psychological autonomy

4. Research that has investigated parental influence during adolescence has revealed that
   a. parental and peer values usually become fundamentally different during adolescence.
   b. parents have very little influence on their children's choice of peer groups.
   c. parental and peer values are not usually fundamentally different during adolescence.
   d. both "a" and "b" are true.

5. According to Erikson, the central task of adolescence is
   a. identity formation.
   b. developing romantic interests in the opposite sex.
   c. acquiring adult skills through part-time or full-time employment.
   d. excelling in school.

6. Adolescents who never develop a strong, clear sense of identity and who often have low self-esteem and immature moral reasoning are in a period of
   a. identity foreclosure.
   b. identity achievement.
   c. identity separation.
   d. identity diffusion.

7. Adolescents who do not engage in a period of questioning and exploration are experiencing
   a. identity foreclosure.
   b. identity achievement.
   c. identity separation.
   d. identity diffusion.

8. Piaget referred to the period during which children view rules as rigid, fixed and unchanging as the stage of
   a. moral realism.
   b. moral relativism.
   c. moral foreclosure.
   d. postconventional morality.

9. According to Kohlberg, an individual whose moral thinking and behavior are guided by self-chosen ethical principles rather than socially regulated rules and laws is reasoning at the
   a. preconventional level.
   b. conventional level.
   c. postconventional level.
   d. unconventional level.

10. Research investigating possible gender differences in moral reasoning has revealed
    a. males score higher on measures of moral reasoning than females.
    b. females score higher on measures of moral reasoning than males.
    c. no significant differences between males and females on measures of moral reasoning.
    d. males are more empathic and females are more justice-oriented in their moral reasoning.

TRUE AND FALSE QUESTIONS: Read the following statements and indicate whether you think each statement is true or false.

1. Children are less prone to conflict with their parents as they grow into adolescence.

2. Studies indicate that parent and peer values are not usually fundamentally different during adolescence.

3. Opportunities for separateness in family interactions are important for girls' identity formation, while connectedness in family relations is especially important for males.

4. Recent studies indicate that children are not capable of understanding another's intention as early as Piaget proposed.

5. The majority of individuals reach either stage five or six on Kohlberg's measure of moral reasoning by adulthood.

6. Studies have revealed that adolescents who work full- or part-time perform better in school and are less likely to be involved in drugs, alcohol and other problem behaviors.

7. According to Erikson, the central task of adolescence is the development of romantic relationships with the opposite sex.

8. Males usually score higher than females on measures of moral reasoning.

9. Studies reveal that preconventional thinking and reasoning decline sharply with age.

10. Young children's moral judgments are not related to resistance, cheating or violation of social norms.

FILL-IN-THE-BLANKS: Read the following sentences and write the missing word or words in the space provided.

1. When children become adolescents, their _____ of their parents changes; they spend _____ time with their parents; and they are more prone to _____ with their parents.

2. When asked what aspects of an adolescent's life parents had authority over, both parents and adolescents agreed that parents had authority over _____ and _____ issues. Most adolescents report that behavior related to _____, _____ choices and _____ choices are within their own personal jurisdiction.

3. Conformity to peer group pressure may be affected by adolescents' _____ background, their relationship with their _____ and other adults, their _____ environment, their _____ , their _____, and their _____ with peers.

4. In adolescence, the components of authoritative parenting consist of _____, _____ supervision and monitoring, and granting of psychological _____.

5. Studies reveal that authoritative parenting has been positively associated with _____ achievement and greater involvement in _____ activities.

6. According to Erikson, the central task of adolescence is _____. Erikson referred to the period of questioning and exploration as a _____ period.

7. Adolescents experiencing _____ do not engage in the period of questioning and exploration. The identity status of adolescents who never develop a strong, clear sense of identity is classified as _____. Adolescents who have a strong sense of who they are after a period of active searching and exploration have attained _____.

8. According to Piaget, in the stage of _____, children believe that rules are handed down by authorities and that rules are _____, _____ and _____. Beginning at age 10 or 11, children enter the stage of _____, and realize that many social rule can be changed by _____ and _____.

9. According to Kohlberg, children at the _____ level of moral reasoning judge right and wrong primarily by the consequences of actions. Individuals at the _____ level focus on interpersonal relationships and social values which take precedence over _____ interests. At the _____ level, moral judgments are based on broad _____ principles rather than because society thinks they are right or wrong.

10. Critics of Kohlberg's research argue that morality is _____ relative and that it is _____ to view one kind of moral thought as higher than another. Critics also charge that Kohlberg's scoring system is biased in favor of _____ because high scores depend on an orientation toward _____.

ANSWERS TO PRACTICE TEST ITEMS

MIX-AND-MATCH

1. f	2. j
3. h	4. i
5. a	6. k
7. c	8. e
9. d	10. l
11. b	12. g

MULTIPLE CHOICE

1. b	2. c
3. d	4. c
5. a	6. d
7. a	8. a
9. c	10. c

TRUE AND FALSE

1. false	2. true
3. true	4. false
5. false	6. false
7. false	8. false
9. true	10. true

FILL-IN-THE-BLANKS

1. perception; less; conflict
2. moral; conventional; friendship; personal; prudential
3. socioeconomic; parents; school; personality; age; status
4. warmth; behavioral; autonomy
5. academic; school
6. identity formation; moratorium
7. identity foreclosure; identity diffusion; identity achievement
8. moral realism; fixed; absolute; sacred; moral relativism; agreement; consensus
9. preconventional; conventional; individual; postconventional; abstract
10. culturally; ethnocentric; males; justice

CHAPTER 16:
DEVELOPMENTAL PSYCHOPATHOLOGY

CHAPTER OVERVIEW

Developmental psychopathology focuses on the origin of psychological and behavioral disorders in children. According to the available data, about one in five children are diagnosed as suffering from some kind of disturbance at some point, although the number of children with persistent problems is probably somewhat lower. Recent studies using behavioral checklists indicate that behavioral and emotional problems may be worsening for children in the United States. Although psychological disturbances during childhood may dissipate over time, serious problems are likely to continue in later life. Studies indicate that psychological intervention and treatment can be effective in eliminating psychological disturbances in children, particularly behavioral methods such as skills training, relaxation training and modeling. Moreover, therapists report that they are equally successful in treating problems of overcontrol and undercontrol in children.

Many of the psychological problems in childhood are related to problems of undercontrol. Children diagnosed with ADHD tend to be physically restless, have difficulty following through on tasks and often act impulsively. Possible causes include neurological, biochemical, social and cognitive factors, although its actual cause is still unknown. Conduct disorders are antisocial behaviors that may or may not be illegal, such as stealing, truancy and fighting. Studies reveal an increase in juvenile offenses in the 1990s, particularly for serious offenses such as violent crimes. Factors that may be associated with juvenile crime include biological influences, personality, parental inadequacy, peer influence and a variety of social factors. It is important to recognize that genetic and environmental factors often interact and that individuals who engage in antisocial acts early in childhood may have biological predispositions that make them vulnerable to adverse environments. Because antisocial behaviors often have multiple causes, efforts to treat delinquency are not very successful. Current research indicates preventative measures may be far more beneficial than punitive measures in the treatment of delinquent behavior.

Although rates of substance abuse have declined in recent years, research exploring its possible causes continues. Studies indicate that negative peer influence, authoritarian and neglecting parenting, and biological susceptibility are all factors that increase the risk of substance abuse in adolescents. For some adolescents, multiple drug use or heavy drug use may reflect emotional disturbances that may have their roots in dysfunctional family relationships.

Some psychological disturbances are problems of overcontrol. Anxiety induces irrational fears and excessive worry in children about problems that are unlikely or remote. Depressive disorders range from mild to severe and may be temporary or long-term. Current research reveals that depression can begin as early as childhood, affecting perhaps as many as 14 percent of the children in the United States. Suicide has increased steadily since the 1960s and is the third leading cause of death in the 15-19-year-old age group. Risk factors include family instability and discord, inability to communicate with parents and early parental loss. Eating disorders such as anorexia and bulimia often emerge during adolescence, are more prevalent in females than in males, and pose serious health risks that may require psychological intervention and treatment.

Autism occurs in two to five children out of 10,000 and is characterized by deviant learning patterns, rigid and unimaginative play, obsessions with certain kinds of objects, and abnormal patterns of social interaction. Current research is exploring possible biological and neurological causes of autism. Although schizophrenia is relatively rare, it is the most common psychotic disorder of adolescence. The incidence of schizophrenia increases significantly after the age of 15 and is characterized by distortions in thinking and language and inappropriate emotional responses. Though its causes are unknown, research indicates that biological factors play an important role.

CHAPTER OUTLINE: Use the outline provided below by writing information related to each topic in the margins of the outline, e.g., definitions of terms and elaboration of concepts.

I. **Studying Problems in Development**

   A. *Taking a developmental perspective*

   B. *Types of emotional disturbance*

   C. *Prevalence of emotional disturbance*

   D. *Duration of emotional disturbance over time*

   E. *Effectiveness of psychotherapy with children*

II. **Problems of Undercontrol**

   A. *Attention deficit hyperactivity disorder*

   B. *Conduct disorders and delinquency*

   C. *Substance abuse*

III. **Problems of Overcontrol**

   A. *Anxiety*

   B. *Depression*

   C. *Suicide*

   D. *Eating disorders*

IV. **Major Disorders in Childhood and Adolescence**

   A. *Autism*

   B. *Adolescent schizophrenia*

KEY DEFINITIONS AND TERMS: Define the following concepts and terms Try to provide an example for each word or term you have defined to help clarify its meaning.

Developmental psychopathology:

Prospective study:

Comorbidity:

Externalizing syndromes:

Internalizing syndromes:

Child behavior checklist:

ADHD:

Status offenses:

Conduct disorder:

Anorexia nervosa:

Bulimia:

Infantile autism:

Adolescent schizophrenia:

Below are questions that relate to key concepts and information covered in your textbook. Answer the questions as thoroughly and completely as possible. Try to provide examples to support your answer and to clarify meaning.

1. What is "developmental psychopathology," and what is the preferred method of research in the study of developmental psychopathology?

2. Discuss the changes that have been made in the diagnostic system used by researchers in the field of developmental psychopathology. What are the three categories of developmental psychopathology under which most disorders are classified?

3. What research methods are used to determine the prevalence of emotional disturbance in children and what are the advantages and disadvantages of each method? According to the available data, what percentage of children can be diagnosed with a disturbance at any time?

4. What have studies using the CBCL revealed about the trend of emotional problems in children over the last few years? Are emotional problems lessening or worsening for children in the United States? Are the changes concentrated in one specific area or are they occurring across a broad range? What cross-cultural and cross-ethnic differences has the CBCL revealed?

5. Do children usually "grow out of" emotional problems or do the problems tend to persist over time? Are problems more likely to persist if they arise during the preschool years or if they arise during the elementary school years? Are "externalizing" problems more or less likely to persist into adulthood than "internalizing" problems?

6. How effective is psychotherapy in the treatment of childhood disturbances? What type of therapy or treatment has been shown to be the most effective? Are therapists equally successful treating problems of overcontrol and undercontrol?

7. What are the symptoms of attention deficit hyperactivity disorder and approximately what percentage of children have it? How do the ratios of males vs. females diagnosed with ADHD compare? What are the consequences of ADHD on academic performance and behavioral problems? How is the presence or absence of delinquency related to verbal IQ? What are some of the possible causes of ADHD and how effective are drugs in its treatment?

8. What criteria do psychologists use to diagnose a conduct disorder? What are some of the challenges faced by researchers who study antisocial behavior?

9. Describe the trends of delinquent behavior in the United States since the 1960s. Has the incidence of serious offenses increased or decreased? What percent of arrests for violent crimes in 1992 were of individuals aged 14 or less? What differences have been reported in the delinquent behavior of males and females?

10. What has research revealed about the possible effect that genetic susceptibility and nongenetic factors, such as perinatal risk, may have on an adolescent's risk for delinquent behavior?

11. Discuss the effect that social and environmental variables may have on an adolescent's risk for delinquent behavior. What has research revealed about the effect that antisocial peers, parental conflict and discipline and parental rejection may have on the development of delinquent behavior during adolescence? How does socioeconomic status affect an adolescent's risk for delinquency?

12. Discuss the interactive effects that biology and environment can have on children's risk for delinquent behavior. What have studies revealed about adopted children who were genetically at risk for delinquency? Did the home environment in which they were raised affect the likelihood of delinquent behavior?

13. Given the multiple causes of delinquent behavior, how successful have been the efforts to treat it? Does imprisonment in traditional "correctional" institutions seem to help? What are the typical reconviction rates among previously institutionalized adolescents? Which method is showing some promise for the treatment of delinquency?

14. Describe current prevalence rates among adolescents in their use of marijuana. Has the use of barbiturates, tranquilizers, inhalants, cocaine, alcohol, and cigarettes increased or decreased? Discuss some of the known causes of substance abuse. What effect do peers, parents, family relationships, and biological susceptibility have on an adolescent's risk for substance abuse?

15. What are some of the characteristics of overanxious children? What percent of children show symptoms of anxiety? Which children appear to be at risk for the development of anxiety problems?

16. Are children capable of becoming depressed? What is the percentage range of childhood depression that has been estimated by various studies? Why are females more prone to depression than males? What are some of the factors associated with childhood depression? What are some of the methods used in the treatment of childhood depression?

17. How common is suicide among children and adolescents? What percent of suicides per 100,000 are committed by people in the 15-19-year-old age group? Are males or females more likely to attempt suicide? Are males or females more likely to complete suicide? What are some of the explanations that have been offered to account for these differences?

18. Discuss some of the reasons for suicide attempts. Why is it important to distinguish between immediate precipitating factors and longer-term predisposing factors? What are some of the risk factors associated with suicide?

19. Cite the signs and symptoms that often precede suicide. Should early warning signs be taken seriously or dismissed and why?

20. Discuss the possible causes of anorexia nervosa and bulimia. What are some of the common personality traits and background variables associated with each of these eating disorders?

21. Describe the symptoms of autism. How many children have been diagnosed with this condition? What are the possible causes of autism that are currently being investigated by researchers?

22. Describe the symptoms of schizophrenia. At what age does the frequency of schizophrenia dramatically increase? What are some of the causal factors associated with schizophrenia and what is its prognosis? Why is it important to distinguish between brief psychotic episodes brought on by reaction to a crisis and schizophrenia?

MIX-AND-MATCH: In the left-hand column below are some key concepts or definitions. Choose the term from the column on the right that best matches each definition provided in the column on the left.

1. Syndromes that are manifested by various kinds of "acting out" behaviors, such as ADHD and delinquency

2. Syndromes that include psychological disorders, such as anxiety, self-deprecation and eating disorders

3. Technique used to study psychopathology that requires parents, teachers, etc., to complete a list of possible problems that may apply to a particular child

4. The preferred method of research in developmental psychopathology in which a group of normal or high-risk children are studied longitudinally

5. Disorder that is characterized by short attention span, physical restlessness, impulsivity, and poor academic performance

6. Term that is used to refer to children and adolescents who exhibit antisocial behavior, whether or not there are laws against the behavior

7. Delinquent acts, such as truancy and curfew violation, that are illegal only when conducted by young people

8. Term that is used to describe children who may have more than one kind of problem

9. Eating disorder that is characterized by self-induced starvation

10. Eating disorder that is characterized by binge eating followed by self-induced vomiting

11. Disorder characterized by a variety of deviant learning patterns, rigid and unimaginative play and deviant patterns of social interactions

12. Disorder characterized by disconnected or incoherent speech, withdrawal, confusion, hallucinations, and inappropriate emotional reactions

a. ADHD

b. Comorbidity

c. Externalizing syndromes

d. Conduct disorder

e. Child behavior checklist

f. Infantile autism

g. Adolescent schizophrenia

h. Bulimia

i. Anorexia nervosa

j. Prospective study

k. Internalizing syndromes

l. Status offenses

MULTIPLE CHOICE QUESTIONS: Read the following questions and indicate your answer by marking the option that you think best answers each question.

1. Externalizing problems typically refer to problems of
   a. overcontrol.
   b. undercontrol.
   c. schizophrenia.
   d. infantile autism.

2. A disadvantage of the child behavior checklist is that
   a. it cannot be used to follow children over long periods of time.
   b. it is not sensitive to cross-cultural and cross-ethnic differences in psychopathology.
   c. it is a more difficult and expensive method than traditional interview methods.
   d. it may not identify children with problems that would trigger a psychiatric diagnosis.

3. The most promising method in the treatment of juvenile delinquency is
   a. behavioral treatment.
   b. educational programs.
   c. foster home placement.
   d. psychotherapy.

4. What percent of arrests for violent crimes in the United States were of individuals aged 14 or less?
   a. 25 percent
   b. 30 percent
   c. 45 percent
   d. 55 percent

5. The earliest that depression has been diagnosed is during
   a. infancy.
   b. childhood.
   c. puberty.
   d. adolescence.

6. Which of the following has not been offered to explain why girls are more likely than boys to become depressed?
   a. Girls are "cognitively weaker" than boys.
   b. Girls are more likely to have worries about their body image than boys.
   c. Girls have a greater likelihood of suffering from forms of sexual abuse.
   d. Girls may experience more pressure to conform to restrictive social roles than boys.

7. Suicide accounts for approximately _____ deaths per 100,000 people in the 15-19-year-old age group.
   a. 11
   b. 15
   c. 23
   d. 37

8. Which of the following is not an early warning sign of suicide?
   a. eating and sleeping disorders
   b. declining school performance
   c. a history of previous suicide attempts
   d. increasing amount of time spent with peers

9. Which of the following is <u>not</u> a symptom of schizophrenia?
   a. disordered thinking
   b. limited capacity for establishing meaningful relationships
   c. obsessions with certain kinds of objects, such as shiny rocks
   d. poor emotional control

10. Which of the following has been ruled out as a possible cause of autism?
    a. genetic factors
    b. deficient mothering
    c. abnormalities in certain parts of the brain
    d. all of the above have been ruled out

TRUE AND FALSE QUESTIONS: Read the following statements and indicate whether you think each statement is true or false.

1. Problems that arise during the preschool years are more likely to persist over several years than problems that arise in the elementary school years.

2. Behavioral treatments have been found to be more effective than "traditional" therapies in the treatment of childhood disorders.

3. Drug treatment has been shown to have positive, long-term benefits for children diagnosed with ADHD.

4. In 1992, 30 percent of arrests for violent crimes in the United States were committed by individuals aged 14 or less.

5. Research has ruled out genetic factors as a possible cause of juvenile delinquency.

6. Imprisonment in traditional correctional institutions has been shown to significantly reduce juvenile delinquency.

7. Efforts to treat delinquency with psychotherapy, foster home placement, recreational programs, and educational and vocational programs have been very successful.

8. Statistics reveal that the overall rate of drug use by adolescents increased significantly from 1979 through 1992.

9. Suicide is the third highest cause of death for people in the 15-19-year-old age group.

10. Autism can now be treated and cured through a combination of drugs and behavioral therapy.

FILL-IN-THE-BLANKS: Read the following sentences and write the missing word or words in the space provided.

1. The psychological approach to understand disturbances in development is referred to as _____. In the past, if researchers did look at developmental history, it was _____. The preferred method currently used in the study of developmental psychopathology is the _____, in which a group of children are studied _____.

273

2. The many specific problems of children fall into three broad categories: _____ problems, or problems of undercontrol; _____ problems, or problems of overcontrol; and major developmental _____, sometimes called psychoses.

3. Children diagnosed with ADHD tend to be physically _____, have great difficulty paying attention to and following through on _____, and often behave _____.

4. The term _____ is a legal phrase that refers to a young person, generally under the age of _____, who engages in behavior that is punishable by law. The term _____ applies to acts such as curfew violation and truancy that are only illegal when committed by young people. The term _____ refers to children and adolescents who exhibit antisocial behavior, whether or not there are laws against it.

5. When considering suicide attempts, it is important to distinguish between immediate _____ events, such as the breakup of a romance, pregnancy, and school failure, and _____ predisposing factors, such as a long history of escalating family instability and discord.

6. Some of the warning signs of suicide include a persistently _____ mood; eating and _____ disturbances; declining performance in _____; increasing _____ from others; a breakdown in _____ with parents; and a previous history of suicide attempts or involvement in _____.

7. The symptoms of autism include a variety of deviant _____ patterns; rigid and unimaginative kinds of _____, coupled with _____ with certain kinds of objects; a rigid insistence on following certain _____; and deviant patterns of social _____.

8. The symptoms of schizophrenia include disordered _____; distortion of, or lack of contact with _____; limited capacity for establishing meaningful _____; and poor _____ control.

9. Overanxious children _____ a great deal about unrealistic possibilities; they are difficult to _____, often have many _____ complaints, and are often tense and find it difficult to _____.

10. One reason why girls may be more vulnerable to depression is that they are more likely than boys to have worries about their _____ images; a second stressor for women is that they have an increased likelihood of suffering from forms of _____ abuse; a third factor is that girls may experience more pressure to conform to a restrictive social _____ than boys.

ANSWERS TO PRACTICE TEST ITEMS

MIX-AND-MATCH

1. c	2. k
3. e	4. j
5. a	6. d
7. l	8. b
9. i	10. h
11. f	12. g

MULTIPLE CHOICE

1. b	2. d
3. a	4. b
5. b	6. a
7. a	8. d
9. c	10. b

TRUE AND FALSE

1. false	2. true
3. false	4. true
5. false	6. false
7. false	8. false
9. true	10. false

FILL-IN-THE-BLANKS

1. developmental psychopathology; retrospective; prospective; longitudinally
2. externalizing; internalizing; deviations
3. restless; tasks; impulsively
4. juvenile delinquent; 18; status offense; conduct disorder
5. precipitating; longer-term
6. depressing; sleeping; school; isolation; communication; accidents
7. learning; play; obsessions; rituals; interactions
8. thinking; reality; relationships; emotional
9. worry; reassure; physical; relax
10. body; sexual; roles